MILES TO GO

The Spiritual Quest of Aging

EDGAR CAYCE'S WISDOM FOR THE NEW AGE

General Editor: Charles Thomas Cayce
Project Editor: A. Robert Smith

Dreams: Tonight's Answers for Tomorrow's Questions,
   Mark Thurston

Awakening Your Psychic Powers, Henry Reed

Reincarnation: Claiming Your Past, Creating Your Future,
   Lynn Elwell Sparrow

Healing Miracles: Using Your Body Energies,
   William A. McGarey, M.D.

Mysteries of Atlantis Revisited, Edgar Evans Cayce, Gail Cayce
   Schwartzer, and Douglas G. Richards

Growing Through Personal Crisis, Harmon Hartzell Bro, with June
   Avis Bro

Soul-Purpose: Discovering and Fulfilling Your Destiny, Mark
   Thurston

Miles to Go: The Spiritual Quest of Aging, Richard Peterson

MILES TO GO

The Spiritual Quest of Aging

RICHARD PETERSON

With a Foreword by Charles Thomas Cayce

1817

Harper & Row, Publishers, San Francisco

New York, Grand Rapids, Philadelphia, St. Louis
London, Singapore, Sydney, Tokyo

For permission to reprint copyrighted material, grateful acknowledgment is made to the following: Bantam Books for passages from *Getting Well Again* by O. Carl Simonton, M.D., Stephanie Matthews-Simonton, and James Creighton (Copyright © 1978 by O. Carl Simonton and Stephanie Matthews-Simonton); Doubleday for passages from *Our Best Years* by Helen Hayes with Marion Glasserow Gladney (Copyright © 1984 by Helen Hayes and Marion Glasserow Gladney); Crown Publishers, Inc., for passages from *Reincarnation: The Phoenix Fire Mystery* compiled and edited by Joseph Head and S. L. Cranston (Copyright © 1977 by Joseph Head and S. L. Cranston); Random House, Inc., for passages from *Memories, Dreams, Reflections* by C. G. Jung (Copyright © 1961, 1962, 1963 by Random House, Inc.) and from *Oh, to Be Fifty Again* by Eda LeShan (Copyright © 1986 by Eda LeShan); Alfred A. Knopf, Inc., for passages from *The Seasons of a Man's Life* by Daniel J. Levinson et al. (Copyright © 1978 by Daniel J. Levinson); Jeremy P. Tarcher, Inc., for passages from *Who Gets Sick* by Blair Justice (Copyright © 1988 by Blair Justice); W. W. Norton & Company, Inc., for passages from *Vital Involvement in Old Age* by Erik H. Erikson, Joan M. Erikson, and Helen Q. Kivnick (Copyright © 1986 by Joan M. Erikson, Erik H. Erikson, Helen Kivnick); William Morrow and Company, Inc., for an excerpt from pp. 25–27 of *Growing Old, Staying Young* by Christopher Hallowell (Copyright © 1985 by Christopher Hallowell); E. P. Dutton, a division of NAL Penguin, Inc., for brief quotes from *Passages: Predictable Crises of Adult Life* by Gail Sheehy (Copyright © 1974, 1976 by Gail Sheehy); and Viking Penguin, Inc., for an excerpt from *A View from Eighty* by Malcolm Cowley (Copyright © 1976, 1978, 1980 by Malcolm Cowley).

FIRST EDITION

Library of Congress Cataloging-in-Publication Data

Peterson, Richard, 1928–
    Miles to go: the spiritual quest of aging / Richard Peterson.
    p.   cm.—(Edgar Cayce's wisdom for the new age)

    Bibliography: p.
    Includes index.
    ISBN 0–06–250676–5 (pbk.)
    1. Aged—Religious life.   2. Aged—Conduct of life.   3. Cayce,
Edgar, 1877–1945.   Edgar Cayce readings.   I. Title.   II. Series.
BL625.4.P48   1989
291.4'48'0240565—dc19   88-43275

89   90   91   92   93   FAIR   10   9   8   7   6   5   4   3   2   1

CONTENTS

LIST OF TABLES

FOREWORD

It is a time in the Earth when people everywhere seek to know more of the mysteries of the mind, the soul," said my grandfather, Edgar Cayce, from an unconscious trance from which he demonstrated a remarkable gift for clairvoyance.

His words are prophetic even today, as more and more Americans in these unsettled times are turning to psychic explanations for daily events. For example, according to a national survey by the National Opinion Research Council, nearly half of American adults today believe they have been in contact with someone who has died, a figure twice that of ten years ago. Two-thirds of all adults say they have had an ESP experience; ten years ago that figure was only one-half.

Every culture throughout history has made note of its own members' gifted powers beyond the five senses. These rare individuals held special interest because they seemed able to provide solutions to life's pressing problems. America in the twentieth century is no exception.

Edgar Cayce was perhaps the most famous and most carefully documented psychic of our time. He began to use his unusual abilities when he was a young man, and from then on for more than forty years he would, usually twice a day, lie on a couch, go into a sleeplike state, and respond to questions. More than fourteen thousand of these discourses, called readings, were carefully transcribed by his secretary and preserved by the Edgar Cayce Foundation in Virginia Beach, Virginia. These psychic readings continue to provide inspiration, insight, and help with healing to tens of thousands of people.

Having only an eighth-grade education, Edgar Cayce lived a plain, simple life by the world's standards. As early as his childhood in Hopkinsville, Kentucky, however, he sensed that he had psychic ability. While alone one day he had a vision of a woman who told him he would have unusual power to help people. He also related experiences of "seeing" dead relatives. Once, while struggling with school lessons, he slept on his spelling book and awakened knowing the entire contents of the book.

As a young man he experimented with hypnosis to treat a recurring throat problem that caused him to lose his speech. He discovered that under hypnosis he could diagnose and describe treatments for the physical ailments of others, often without knowing or even seeing the person with the ailment. People began to ask him other sorts of questions, and he found himself able to answer these as well.

In 1910 the *New York Times* published a two-page story with pictures about Edgar Cayce's psychic ability as described by a young physician, Wesley Ketchum, to a clinical research society in Boston. From that time on people from all over the country with every conceivable question sought his help.

In addition to his unusual talents, Cayce was a deeply religious man who taught Sunday school all of his adult life and read the entire Bible once for every year that he lived. He always tried to attune himself to God's will by studying the Scriptures and maintaining a rich prayer life, as well as by trying to be of service to those who came seeking help. He used his talents only for helpful purposes. Cayce's simplicity and humility and his commitment to doing good in the world continue to attract people to the story of his life and work and to the far-reaching information he gave.

In this series we hope to provide the reader with insights in the search for understanding and meaning in life. Each book in the series explores its subject from the viewpoint of the Edgar Cayce readings, comparing it with the perspectives of other metaphysical literature and of current scientific thought. The interested reader needs no prior knowledge of the Cayce information. When one of the Edgar Cayce readings is quoted, the identifying number of that reading is included for those who wish to read the full text. Each volume includes suggestions for further study.

This book, *Miles to Go: The Spiritual Quest of Aging*, by Richard Peterson, Ph.D., draws upon the many suggestions found in the Cayce readings for dealing positively with the natural process of maturing, and for living a life of meaning at any age. The author also uses collaborative information from recent scientific findings concerning the mystery of longevity and living a healthy life. As former manager of human resources for the Association for Research and Enlightenment, Dr. Peterson has spent years working with the Cayce material and working with people of all ages. He is superbly qualified to write this book, which should prove helpful to anyone interested in growing older with vitality and purpose.

Charles Thomas Cayce, Ph.D.
President
Association for Research and Enlightenment

PREFACE

This book is addressed to readers of any age who want to make the most of the miles ahead of them in their elder years—their sixties, seventies, eighties, and beyond. This includes those in their middle years who want to prepare for the years ahead, as well as those already in their elder years who will accept more from life than they are now experiencing. Those of any age who will apply the ideas and suggestions in this book to their daily lives will discover more purpose in life and greater satisfaction with themselves and their circumstances than they might have imagined possible. They will experience positive changes in physical well-being, in mental enrichment, and in spiritual fulfillment. I do not make this promise lightly.

One sign of the growing interest in life in the elder years is the increasing number of books and articles about age and aging—the process of aging, coping with your age or enjoying your age (whichever it is), caring for the aging, and on and on. So why another book? One unique contribution of this book is the material that is its foundation—the psychic readings given by Edgar Cayce in his efforts to help hundreds of individuals deal with their physical, mental, and spiritual concerns. Some of those concerns related directly to the process of growing older, but many more related to the broader prospect of living a meaningful, useful life regardless of age. I have drawn upon a wide selection of Cayce readings in developing suggestions for growing old with confidence and grace. Very simply, my purpose is to demonstrate how the life of the later years can be vitalized by applying ideas expressed in the philosophy represented by the Cayce readings.

According to Malcolm Cowley, poet, essayist, and critic, in his book *The View from 80*, I am one of many authors dealing with the topic of aging who are but "lads and lasses . . . in their late fifties and early sixties." He suggests that we may know the literature, "but not the life. . . . What they didn't and couldn't know was how it feels to be old." I have attempted to compensate partly for my youthful "view from sixty" by talking with people who have the advantage of being in their sixties, seventies, and eighties. My ten conversation partners do not represent a random sample of aging Americans, but instead are individuals who try to live according to a philosophy of life represented in the Edgar Cayce readings.

This book is presented in a format that encourages you to act on the ideas presented. Many Edgar Cayce readings remind the individuals getting the readings that they must apply the information they receive in the readings before they can experience change for the better. Experimenting with new ideas is one way to start converting knowledge to wisdom and to begin experiencing the fulfillment of my earlier promise. Throughout the book are segments labeled "Getting Personal" that include inventories and other activities designed to move the ideas out of the book and into your life. I recommend you start a notebook, a kind of personal journal, in which to complete the exercises and keep other kinds of relevant notes. Use it to record and celebrate growth, to identify and resolve problems, and to plan future action. I firmly believe you will find such a notebook a valuable companion as you experiment with the ideas and suggestions. If you have a spouse or close friend who shares your life, I suggest you offer him or her the opportunity to participate with you in the recommended exercises and activities. My promise is valid for both of you.

May you find vitality, wisdom, and grace in the miles ahead!

ACKNOWLEDGMENTS

In his readings Edgar Cayce frequently mentioned that the service one person provided to another was "the highest service to God." In a reading for one individual he said that service to someone else was the *only* way to bring contentment to life and to find joy in living.

Many individuals have been of service to me in the preparation of this book and should share in the satisfaction of its completion. My special appreciation and love are expressed to these:

My soulmate, marriage partner, first editor, and best friend, Anita, who enriches my own life with Spirit, and without whom I might never have heard of Edgar Cayce.

My ten "conversation partners" and dear friends, who have helped extend my vision of the mature life with Spirit: Ada, Belva, Don, Dora Lou, Everett, Mae, Mike, Nell, Richard, and Shane.

My parents, Lea and Oscar, who have been models for growing old gracefully, and now at 87 and 92 provide remarkable models of love and companionship in the elder years.

My mother-in-law, Alice, whose very presence at 85 is a reminder of the quiet strength of kindness and gentleness.

My children and grandchildren, Scott, Fran, Lyn, Kelsey, and Holly, who symbolize the ongoing flow of love and support through new generations.

My deep thanks is also extended to the following: Mark Thurston, whose writings, lectures, and leadership have significantly influenced my own work with the Edgar Cayce readings; Charles Thomas Cayce, who has provided constant support, ongoing encouragement, and opportunities for my work; Bob Smith, whose editorial guidance and moral support kept me on course; and especially Edgar Cayce himself, whose extraordinary legacy of the readings and whose organization have transformed my life.

To all these individuals I dedicate this book with love.

But I have promises to keep,
And miles to go before I sleep.

ROBERT FROST
From "Stopping by Woods on a Snowy Evening"

PART I

Before I Sleep

INTRODUCTION TO PART I

Before I Sleep

To be seventy years young is sometimes far more cheerful and hopeful than to be forty years old.

OLIVER WENDELL HOLMES at eighty, in a letter to Julia Ward Howe on her seventieth birthday, May 27, 1889

It's not how old you are, but how you are old.

MARIE DRESSLER at sixty-five, as quoted in *Reader's Digest*, March 1934

Most people say that as you get old, you have to give up things. I think you get old because you give up things.

SENATOR THEODORE FRANCIS GREEN at eighty-seven, as quoted in the *Washington Post*, June 28, 1954

GETTING OLDER IS BOTH a fact and a perception. Even if you don't turn calendar pages every day, you cannot be unaware of the passage of time. With each passing day you are one day older. Yet haven't you noticed that not all minutes or hours seem equal? Don't you feel that some days or weeks are longer than others?

Your views about your lifetime and where you are in it have

emerged from many influences—parents, teachers, religious leaders, friends, books, newspapers, movies, television. Whatever age you may be, if you consider your perceptions of life and of the world around you, you will probably discover that your particular view of reality—your personal paradigm—is not much different from the views of others around you. This paradigm is your basis for considering questions such as, What is life on this planet all about? Is the world around me real or an illusion created by my mind? Is there a purpose for my being on this planet with my mind and my feelings, or is the human an accident of biological evolution? Is there any unique purpose for my life?

As long as you stick to one simple paradigm, especially one on which you were raised, you can answer (or ignore) these questions with relative comfort and consistency. The price for that simplicity, however, is that you also have to accept the consequences that accompany that paradigm, that view of reality. If your paradigm allows you to believe that life is primarily for achieving the greatest material gain or personal happiness for yourself, for example, and is without any ultimate purpose, then you must be prepared to accept feelings of despair and meaninglessness that may appear in your later years.

Chapter 1 summarizes some of the conditions and limitations of a conventional paradigm of the Western world. It gives readers the opportunity to test the boundaries of their own views relating to the process of aging as they see it around them and experience it in themselves.

Chapter 2 presents concepts from a paradigm less conventional among people growing up in Western civilizations—ideas and principles found in the Edgar Cayce readings. These concepts are not as alien to the Western mind today as they were just a few years ago. Expression of these ideas is becoming more commonplace, although sometimes they are spoken of in a skeptical, humorous, or even derogatory way, just as other new ideas threatening old paradigms have often faced criticism or derision.

Cautious readers may elect to suspend judgment temporarily about concepts that are outside their current comfortable paradigms. After trying out some of the ideas presented in the book, however, even skeptical readers may find their views moving in the direction of the new concepts. Or they may discover that, once they are convinced about the benefits of using those ideas, they can accept and apply many of the principles and techniques of those ideas while remaining substantially within their present paradigms.

1

"Almost Too Late?": A View Through "Conventional Eyes"

All would live long, but none would be old.
BENJAMIN FRANKLIN, *Poor Richard's Almanack*, 1749

Have you ever felt, "I can't believe I'm going to be forty next month" . . . or fifty . . . or sixty? Few events in our adult lives are the subject of so many jokes and jibes as our encounters with decade birthdays. For some of us these special birthdays stir up anxiety in the anticipation and resentment in the passage. The occasions often prompt us to examine the quality of our lives—to measure ourselves against some ill-defined but elevated standard for "living the good life." We evaluate our choices of daily work, our style of living, our relationships, our resources.

To illustrate: I recently attended a surprise party for a woman turning "nifty fifty," according to a balloon floating near the ceiling. Looking back, she was thankful to have survived several painful years of health and family challenges. Looking ahead, she felt some urgency to step up the pace of her career in art, now that she was plunging into her fifties.

When young adults reach their first "big one" at thirty, they ask themselves questions such as, How did I get here so soon? Am I heading in the right direction? What have I been doing with my life? What am I missing out on?

In *The Seasons of a Man's Life*, psychologist Daniel Levinson writes:

> To a person in the twenties, it appears that passing 30 is getting "over the hill." In the thirties, turning 40 is a powerful threat. At every point in life, the passing of the next age threshold is anticipated as a total loss of youth, of vitality and of life itself. What can it mean, then, to approach 60 and to feel that all forms of youth . . . are about to disappear, so that only "old age" remains?

One answer to this question, says Levinson, is to find at every life stage a balance between the values of youth and the values of age. In late adulthood, for example, he suggests we can move toward the image of the "creative, wise elder" while retaining the "connection to youthful vitality, to the forces of growth in self and world." As we grow older we can minimize the anxieties about lost youth if we live dynamically by continuing to develop our inner resources and by applying those resources in our outer lives. The Edgar Cayce readings provide a wide range of guidance for bringing such vitality into our lives.

In their landmark research on the developmental cycles of adulthood, Levinson and his associates at Yale identified four eras into which lives are divided with remarkable consistency. Overlapping with the end of one era and the beginning of the next are three major transitional periods. The third and last of these is the late Adult Transition, usually occurring between the ages of sixty and sixty-five. Levinson considers this transition a "period of significant development" that "represents a major turning point in the life cycle." Notice he uses the word *development*, not *decline* or *decay*.

An essential task in each transitional period is an appraisal that asks, What have I done so far and where do I go from here? Individuals who give no thought to questions such as these in the transitional period are less likely to adjust effectively to the next era. In fact, they may try to continue operating at the level of the preceding period, thus accounting for the thirty-five-year-old who still doesn't know what he wants to be when he grows up, as well as for the seventy-year-old still trying to hang onto a set of midlife ambitions and expectations. The transitional period is a means for people to distance themselves from the past while preparing for the future.

Another classic study of human development is the research by psychoanalyst Erik Erikson observing the lives of several families over many years. In *Childhood and Society*, published in 1950, Erikson identifies eight ages of human development from infancy through old age, each of which is fundamental to normal psychosocial development and each of which is characterized by a unique set of choices to make and issues to resolve. In a recent book, *Vital Involvement in Old Age*, Erikson concentrates on people in his eighth age—old age—and what it takes to achieve a satisfactory integration of all that has come before, "to consolidate a sense of wisdom with which to live out the future."

In brief, both the Erikson and the Levinson studies suggest that there is no better time than the mature years to undertake the kind of self-analysis we used to reserve for our earlier decade birthdays—where have we been, how does it all fit together, and where do we go from here? Ideas suggested by the Edgar Cayce readings can help us weather the sixty-to-sixty-five transition period with grace. And more than that, the readings offer much to enrich the subsequent years of life—the elder years.

THE YEARS BEHIND YOU

The primary focus of this book is the period ahead of you—the later years of your life. But to give perspective to the future—and especially to the viewpoint of the next chapter—I will take a brief look at the past through the eyes of the present.

Near one of the later decade markers, you may feel, "If I haven't done it yet, I will probably never do it." For some, that may happen as early as fifty; for others, it may be more like seventy or even eighty; and for still others, such giving up may never take place.

It is not unusual to become discouraged about the years behind you—often a result of perceiving the differences between what you had hoped and planned for, and what actually happened. Unmet expectations constitute probably your single greatest cause of frustration, disappointment, and even despair. You tend to measure your mental and physical accomplishments against those of others and against absolutes, rather than looking at yourself for your own gains and improvements. You tend to look at the material things you have or haven't acquired, rather than at the lives you have touched favorably or the services you have performed.

You may be like the character George Bailey, portrayed by James Stewart in the film classic *It's a Wonderful Life!* When George hits a low of despair, he almost jumps off a bridge in an attempt to end it all. But a kindly novice angel named Clarence stops him and shows him how much he has contributed to his town of Bedford Falls, to his family, and to the lives of people around him—people to whom he gave financial support, a second chance, or an opportunity to make an honest living. According to the Cayce readings, perhaps your greatest accomplishments in life are experiences in which you help others recover from a stumble or help them take the next step forward in their lives.

Throughout this book are exercises and activities headed "Getting Personal," designed to help you apply the ideas from the book directly to your life. A frequent reminder by Edgar Cayce's source to those receiving readings is that in the application comes the understanding. As suggested in the preface, you may wish to start a notebook for completing the exercises in this book and for recording your ideas and plans.

GETTING PERSONAL

Take a few minutes to think back over your life, concentrating on the past twenty years or so. List some of your accomplishments in terms of:

services performed	opportunities taken
products completed	goals reached
skills or knowledge learned	experiences gained
people helped	creativity released

Assume that your angel is standing beside you pointing out how you have made the world a different place in your own special way. What would not have gotten done except for you? Whose life have you made better for your being in it? What lessons have you learned that you could pass on to others?

Don't weigh or measure your accomplishments. Don't dwell on incompleteness, slow starts, or goals not achieved. The Cayce readings advise us that we fail only if we quit trying. So just write down your accomplishments and enjoy them!

It's time to stop reading and start writing your list. When you are finished, set your notes aside. You will refer to them later.

WHERE NOW IS

You've looked backward; now refocus on the present. Specifically, look at one aspect of your personal view of the world—your current ideas and attitudes about life in the later years.

Your perceptions about life after sixty or seventy or eighty have developed from public sources (such as news articles, television programs, and books) and from personal sources (such as aging relatives and friends). On the one hand, you may admire the accomplishment of living to an advanced age—"You're eighty-five? That's marvelous!" On the other hand, you may express amazement that a vital life is possible at such an age—"How does he continue to conduct an orchestra at eighty-nine?" In other words, your paradigm has you believe that living to an advanced age is remarkable, and that functioning effectively at such an age is next to unbelievable!

Henry Wadsworth Longfellow recognized this ambivalence and responded with a short catalog of elder year accomplishments in his poem "Morituri Salutamus":

> *It is too late! Ah, nothing is too late*
> *Till the tired heart shall cease to palpitate.*
> *Cato learned Greek at eighty; Sophocles*
> *Wrote his grand Oedipus, and Simonides*

Bore off the prize of verse from his compeers,
When each had numbered more than four-score years.
. . . .

Chaucer, at Woodstock with the nightingales,
At sixty wrote the Canterbury Tales;
Goethe at Weimar, toiling to the last,
Completed Faust when eighty years were past.
These are indeed exceptions; but they show
How far the gulf-stream of our youth may flow
Into the arctic regions of our lives. . . .

Many of your attitudes about aging are encapsulated by Ben Franklin's paradox that opened this chapter: you want to live a long time, but you don't want to grow old. In fact, you may shun those who have already done so. Is there any other situation in life where you hope to one day join the very group toward which you may be derogatory?

Let's get personal and look at your ideas about being a senior in society.

GETTING PERSONAL

Table 1, which follows, is a self-inventory by which you can assess what you think it is like to grow older. (The word *elder* is used in the inventory to denote a person in the later years, especially one older than seventy.)

At the right of each statement is a rating scale from "Strongly agree" in the left column to "Strongly disagree" in the right column. Circle the answer in the column that best represents your view of the statement, ignoring for now the value of the number you are circling. Rate each statement according to your sincere belief, not according to what you think the "correct" answer is.

After you complete the self-inventory, score it by adding up the numbers you have circled. Find the total in one of the following ranges:

41–50: You appear to have a very healthy, optimistic view of life

Table 1
Self-Inventory: What Is It Like to Grow Older?

For each statement, circle the answer in the column that best represents your level of agreement or disagreement.

Strongly disagree

Disagree

Undecided

Agree

Strongly agree

	Strongly agree	Agree	Undecided	Disagree	Strongly disagree
1. As people grow older, their less pleasing personality traits usually become more prominent than their pleasing ones.	1	2	3	4	5
2. Regularly exercising the mind and the memory can help them function more effectively.	5	4	3	2	1
3. When elders try to learn new skills or knowledge, they set themselves up for disappointment.	1	2	3	4	5
4. Looking back over life from the later years is not especially useful or mentally healthy.	1	2	3	4	5
5. Diet is less important in later years, because the body and its health are so much the product of past diet.	1	2	3	4	5
6. An employer of office workers older than 70 can expect to see their productivity decline steadily.	1	2	3	4	5
7. Those elders who have not had a previous interest in personal growth or spiritual devlopment can still accomplish a lot in the later years.	5	4	3	2	1
8. Elders' new friends should primarily be others in their later years.	1	2	3	4	5
9. People will probably live longer if they reduce their involvement with outside activities in the later years.	1	2	3	4	5
10. People's mental attitude about growing older has an impact on their physical well-being as they age.	5	4	3	2	1

in the later years. You have avoided most of the stereotypes that tend to represent elder people as limited in capability, narrow in interests, inflexible in attitudes and habits, unable to grow and change. Instead, you apparently sense the possibilities for a dynamic life in these years, even if it requires some adjustment and compromise. You recognize that the elder person is quite capable of being flexible and of changing to meet circumstances.

For you, this book confirms your positive outlook on the later years. You have great potential for taking advantage of opportunities and developing strategies for shaping your own future in a positive way.

31–40: You appear to have a generally positive view of life in the later years, although you are not quite ready to give up all stereotypes that represent elder people as somewhat limited in capability, narrow in interests, inflexible in attitudes and habits, and unable to grow and change. You probably hope the stereotypes are untrue so you can enjoy the possibilities of a more dynamic life, even if you must make some adjustments and compromises according to your circumstances.

For you, this book may help dispel your concerns about the later years. You then will have the potential for taking advantage of opportunities and developing strategies for shaping your own future in a positive way.

21–30: You appear to have a somewhat negative view of life in the later years, accepting as true many of the stereotypes that represent elder people as limited in capability, narrow in interests, inflexible in attitudes and habits, and unable to grow and change. You do not see much prospect for living a meaningful, dynamic life in those years, but seem to expect a period of decline, limitation, and isolation.

This book may help you reevaluate your views about the later years and their limitations as you see them. If you are willing to learn and apply some of its techniques, this book can provide you with opportunities and strategies to help you avoid the stereotypical pitfalls and shape your own future in a more positive way.

10–20: You appear to have a very negative view of living in the later years, accepting as true most stereotypes that represent elder people as limited in capability, narrow in interests, inflexible in attitudes and habits, and unable to grow and change. Apparently you see no prospect for living a meaningful, dynamic life in those years, and fully expect that period to be one of decline, limitation, and isolation.

This book will help you reevaluate your views about the later years and their limitations as you see them. If you can set some of your current views and priorities aside while you work with this book and if you will try out some of the book's ideas and techniques, you will discover not only that your views have changed, but also that you are beginning to shape your own future in a more positive way.

———————————

People adopt narrow views about aging when their experience with those in their elder years is limited. And limited experience can lead people to exhibit the prejudice encountered by Sarah-Patton Boyle, who says in her book *The Desert Blooms* that she had become a member of "one undifferentiated entity—*oldpeople*, spelled as one word." What follows such labeling, she points out, is the attachment of "fixed images, or stereotypes, [which] cling to them like tar and feathers."

Such views will change with the increased contact everyone will have with older people as years go by. Population changes are already taking care of this, as we will see.

THE YEARS AHEAD

One reassuring thought goes with being older than sixty-five: whenever it is you get there, you will have a lot more company in your age bracket than sixty-five-pluses did in years past. Back in 1900, for example, only one out of every twenty-five people living was older than sixty-five; in 1987 it was one out of every nine; by the year 2000 it will be one in every five. Obviously, the longer you wait to become sixty-five, the more company you will have.

Another reassurance is that you may have more years ahead of you than you realize. In 1980 there were 14,200 people in the United States one hundred years old or older. By 1985 this had increased a phenomenal 80 percent to 25,400, and could be more than 100,000 by the year 2000. Medical science says the human body seems to be built for a life span of 110 to 120 years, assuming a disease unrelated to age does not strike. The information in the Edgar Cayce readings suggests that the human body could last much longer than it currently does, and that each of us is capable of significantly prolonging his or her life. We need not count ourselves out of the human race when we reach the life expectancy we had when we were born. I recently had a tiny taste of immortality when I discovered I had passed my original life expectancy of 59. Of course the actuaries are clever—as you keep on surviving, they keep raising your life expectancy.

But before you celebrate the possibilities of a long life, you must consider how you would use that life. What would be the purpose of living past one hundred? Mere survival? The satisfaction of outlasting most other human beings? Or do you have something more imaginative and productive in mind?

The possibilities for your later years may be infinite in variety, but limited by your capabilities, resources, and imagination when you get there. I'm going to ask you to think about those later years, whenever they begin (or began) for you. But first, review this list of opportunities:

Take college courses or courses in adult education
Get serious about a craft or hobby
Start a new career as a self-employed person
Find new outside employment
Get more exercise
Get more sleep
Get involved in the care of grandchildren
Take on new volunteer responsibilities

Read the world's one hundred great books
Watch more television (or less television)
Work on your spiritual development
Get serious about gardening or landscaping
Travel widely (or stay at home more)
Learn a new language
Make new friends
Have more of a social life (or less of a social life)

You must have dozens of your own ideas, so now it's time to get personal again.

GETTING PERSONAL

Take a few minutes now to imagine your future, considering your own circumstances, capabilities, and limitations. Write down the decade birthday number and year for each of your next several decade birthdays. Mine for example, are

70 in 1998
80 in 2008 (How exhilarating to pass the year 2000!)
90 in 2018
100 in 2028 (Why not? My dad's in his nineties.)

For each of your upcoming decade birthdays, jot down a few notes on what you would like to be doing at that time, if your circumstances and resources permit it. Where will you be? How will you be spending your time? Who will be with you? What will be giving you the greatest satisfactions in your life?

If you are in a close personal relationship, consider including the other person in your brainstorming about the future. You may answer the questions as a couple, or each of you may answer them separately and then compare notes.

Did you have any feeling that trying to brainstorm your future was "really silly" or "a waste of time"? Maybe you didn't even take the time to do it. Consider this: If you can't articulate reasonable future circumstances for yourself, does that mean you don't care about what actually happens? On the other hand, is it possible to bring into being something you sincerely want?

To answer these questions, another must be asked: How well have you done so far in getting what you plan for? The process of aging is full of surprises from childhood on: you look forward to completing your education, only to find you must never stop learning. You strive for career goals of financial security, satisfying work, and perhaps recognition by others, only to discover much of your time and energy is needed to make even modest gains in these areas. You anticipate a period of stable relationships, a day when you can live off the "income" from the interpersonal "investments" you have made, only to find that such relationships require continual "funding" of your accounts.

So you may conclude that it is not possible to bring what you want into being, that chance or fate or outside circumstances will take over and determine for you what will actually take place. The next chapter will present some ideas based on the Cayce readings that may come head to head with your views on who controls your future, and with other views that you see through your "present eyes." Don't discount new ideas before you really find out about them and perhaps try out some of them. For example, don't decide that wishing is useless. Consider instead that perhaps you should be careful what you wish for, because you may get it!

Are you ready to play "musical viewpoints"? If so, it's time to move over to the next chair while the music of your life plays on.

2

"Never Too Late!": A View Through "New Eyes"

Grow old along with me!
The best is yet to be.
The last of life, for which the first was made:
Our times are in his hand
Who saith, "A whole I planned,
Youth shows but half; trust God: see all, nor be afraid!"
ROBERT BROWNING, *Rabbi Ben Ezra*

As BACKGROUND FOR AN alternative view of aging, open your mind to the following description of why we are here and what we are doing, as suggested by the Cayce readings:

Before memory and time, the infinity of the universe existed in perfection. It consisted of One Energy of high and unchanging vibration—the ultimate Creative Force. To share the universe, the One Energy created a form called soul. The soul was also perfect, its vibration being almost as high as that of the Energy from which it came. In an instant soul creation happened millions of times, each soul as perfect as its Source, each having received the gift of freedom, the potential for individuality. Each soul was created to be a companion to, and cocreator with, the ultimate Creative Force, which is God.

God divided the infinite universe into many realms, all from the same Universal Energy, but differing from one another in their rates of vibration. As the souls moved freely through the universe, they experienced vibratory change as they entered each realm. In some of them they also experienced the limitations of time and memory. They no longer felt their perfection, but began to experience emotions, desires, longings, and lacks. They also experienced the beginning of separation from God. In realms such as Earth, many souls found themselves caught up in the exploration of physical form and mate-riality. These experiences began to have different effects on the souls, some being drawn again and again to Earth and its law of cause and effect.

Every soul has two kinds of memory: soul memory and experi-ence memory. Between realms a soul's soul memory goes back to its creation. Within a realm such as Earth, a soul's experience memory lasts only as long as the soul remains in that realm. Soul memory allows each soul to recall its earliest existence, when it was part of the One Energy, and thus souls recognize they are no longer perfect.

Each soul understands that it can again become an integral part of the One Energy, the Creative Force. Because the experiences in the realms have drawn the souls away from perfection, souls must use those same kinds of experiences to return to God.

The primary means by which progression toward Oneness or regression away from Oneness occurs is through the soul's choices of experiences and actions within those experiences. These choices are made more difficult because of the gifts of individual freedom and will. Once an advance is made along the spiritual path in one expe-rience, however, that advance may be retained in subsequent experi-ences, so growth can continue from one experience to the next. An experience may also prove to be a loss in progress.

After each sojourn, the soul chooses the next experience to pro-vide a new challenge for growth and progression toward Oneness. The attributes it develops in other realms are often tested when it returns to the realm of Earth. And so each soul gradually begins to overcome its separation, to subjugate desire to will, and thus to re-alize its perfection once again. Finally there will be no need to con-tinue its journey from realm to realm. The soul will have achieved

Oneness, becoming again cocreator with the Creative Force, which is God.

You may well wonder how much of the preceding narrative is fiction, how much is allegorical, and how much represents a truth that is simply beyond earthly memory and consciousness. Considered beside the mundane day-to-day details of your life, such a metaphysical idea may seem far removed from reality. And yet that may be only because you are completely absorbed—as you are intended to be—by your current experience in what seems to be your one and only life in the one and only habitable world.

LOOKING BACK WITH NEW EYES

To make this speculative soul view more tangible, let's follow a segment of one soul's path. Although souls have no need for Earth-type names and are androgynous (both male and female), the story will be easier to tell and sound more personal if I talk about a soul with a name—Nam-Ow:

Nam-Ow had begun its spiritual journey back to Oneness, to become a cocreator with the One Force sometimes called God. Part of that journey required lessons for learning patience and forbearance. So Nam-Ow selected an Earth experience in the male physical form of an entity to be known as Porum, born into a family of Jews during their Egyptian exile.

As the transition was made from Nam-ow to Porum, its soul memory was set aside and a new, very primitive Earth memory began. At the age of five, Porum narrowly missed death in a massacre of children by the Egyptians. Experiencing blinding terror and devastating fear, Porum determined never to give in to such emotions again. With his family he followed Moses and Aaron into the wilderness.

Porum grew to manhood, frequently expressing anger over the Jews' lack of progress toward reaching the Promised Land and impatience at the leadership of the elderly Moses. Thus Porum's Earth memory and Earth personality were not aligned with that part of his soul's purpose aimed at learning patience in this experience. Although participation in the traditional prayers and meditations might have helped him get in touch with the purpose of his existence, he refused to take part in the long rituals that constantly delayed their journey. Finally, as a follower of Joshua during the preparations for the siege of Jericho, he was killed by another Jew in an argument over weapons.

So in this Earth sojourn, the soul Nam-Ow lost more ground than it gained on its spiritual journey. Many times Nam-Ow returns to Earth, not only to develop patience, but to learn other lessons, such as cooperation, faith, virtue, understanding, love, and—the most fundamental lesson of all—the Oneness of all energy, all life, all spirit.

The story of Nam-Ow's sojourn on Earth as Porum is comparable to information found in many of the Cayce life readings. In such readings Cayce described in detail several of the appearances on Earth of a specific soul, particularly when those experiences reflected a pattern of lessons being learned. If Edgar Cayce had recounted the Nam-Ow story in a life reading, he might well have concluded, in typical life reading language, "In this experience, the entity lost . . . and lost."

In the aggregate, the Cayce life readings, together with others of his philosophical readings, provide a comprehensive, cohesive, and consistent view of the purpose of life and the soul's journey along the spiritual path. Many people accept this view wholly or in part as a foundation for their personal philosophy. Aging is seen in a different light, of course, if you believe that this lifetime is only one of many.

Before going further with a view through new eyes, it's time to get personal again—to give you a chance to express your position on some of these ideas.

GETTING PERSONAL

This exercise will be most useful if you consider your responses carefully, reflecting in them how you *really* feel about each statement. Don't try to come up with the right answer (there isn't one), but with the answer that truly represents your current belief system.

Table 2
Self-Inventory: The Way of "New Eyes"

For each statement, circle the answer in the column that best represents your current level of agreement or disagreement.

	Strongly disagree	Disagree	Undecided	Agree	Strongly agree
1. People do not have free will.	1	2	3	4	5
2. Dreams are mostly reflections of people's hidden desires and thoughts.	1	2	3	4	5
3. Meditation is primarily a relaxation technique.	1	2	3	4	5
4. People are capable of causing cells in their bodies to regenerate.	5	4	3	2	1
5. Electricity, nuclear power, and the Creative Force we call God are all the same energy.	5	4	3	2	1
6. For most people living today, this is neither the first life on Earth nor the last.	5	4	3	2	1
7. People's unspoken thoughts affect the world around them.	5	4	3	2	1
8. A memory is never completely lost.	5	4	3	2	1
9. Every human being has a specific purpose for living on Earth at this time.	5	4	3	2	1
10. People have little personal responsibility for the circumstances in which they find themselves.	1	2	3	4	5
11. Physical healing can be helped by a strong desire for healing on the part of the person to be healed.	5	4	3	2	1
12. People have chosen, either consciously or subconsciously, all the attitudes they hold.	5	4	3	2	1
13. People have the creative energy of God within them.	5	4	3	2	1
14. People can significantly influence how long they live.	5	4	3	2	1
15. Only a few gifted individuals can develop psychic ability.	1	2	3	4	5

For each of the fifteen statements in Table 2, express your present degree of agreement or disagreement as you did in Table 1.

After you complete the self-inventory, score it by adding up the numbers you have circled. Find the total in one of the following ranges:

56–75: Most of the ideas of the "new eyes" viewpoint seem to be compatible with your current way of thinking. You should be able to apply most of the suggestions in the chapters that follow without making a major shift in your view of reality. Even if you find some specific ideas difficult to accept, your overall orientation is already in the direction I will show you. The information in the self-inventory is discussed at length in the chapters that follow.

35–55: You seem to have mixed feelings or are mostly undecided about the ideas expressed from the "new eyes" viewpoint. If that represents an open mind, then continue to keep your mind open as you apply suggestions in the ensuing chapters. The information in the self-inventory is discussed at length in those chapters, so your questions and concerns will get clarified as you proceed.

15–34: Most of the ideas of the "new eyes" viewpoint seem to be contrary to your current way of thinking. For you to work with and accept some of the ideas presented in this book, you may have to suspend your judgment about the validity of such ideas until you see them in action, until you see how they can make your later years more fulfilling and meaningful. You don't have to buy into all of them in order to find value and benefit in some of them. The information in the self-inventory is discussed at length in the chapters that follow.

————————————————

Your present view of reality—your paradigm—has a largely untraceable history. No one sat down and said, "Now let's develop a plan for how this person will view life and its meaning," and you never stopped to say, "I wonder which view of the world I should accept." Your ideas about the nature of life and the universe may have been shaped by a grandmother who knew all about animals and trees and the changing seasons, a teacher who made the mystery of astronomy contagious, a TV series on modern science and technology, and a succession of ministers who seemed able to separate right from wrong, good from evil, and life from death. Eda LeShan, in *Oh, To Be Fifty Again!* reminds us,

> We define ourselves through parental expectations and the reactions of other people; we define ourselves by sudden new perceptions of our own. And we define ourselves by what the culture tells us rather than what we feel internally.

One element prominent in most personal views of life is the high value placed on youth and youthfulness. Closely tied to that are some traditional perceptions about an inevitable decline of capability in later life and about the finality of death. In the preface to *The Seasons of a Man's Life*, Daniel Levinson says,

> Our overly negative imagery of old age adds greatly to the burden of middle age. It is terrifying to go through middle age in the shadow of death, as though one were already very old.

Our Western model of civilization presents few positive images of growing old. Yet other viewpoints exist, in fact are commonplace, in other modern civilizations, including many Eastern cultures. The readings of Edgar Cayce bring these options to us for our consideration. And as reflected in the work of Levinson, Erikson, and others, there is no better time for personally investigating the ultimate meanings of life than when you approach your later years. And while you are thus taking stock, why not lay the groundwork for some "sudden new perceptions" by exposing yourself to new options for your view of reality?

ALTERNATIVES FOR VIEWING LIFE

Most people do not deliberate about the meaning of life very often or very long: Why am I here? What is the purpose of my life? Does it make any difference in the scheme of things if I accomplish anything during my life? Is there, in fact, any scheme of things? Does God exist? If so, what does God have to do with my life?

A paradigm for an individual brought up in our Western Judeo-Christian culture might go something like this:

In my life there is a divine power I call God. Like a loving parent, he judges what I do as right or wrong, good or evil, keeping score on me. Although I pray to him periodically, I can't say I have a truly personal relationship with him.

I believe God would like us to achieve world peace, interpersonal cooperation and love, and individual happiness. He expects us to achieve these through our own capabilities and free will, applied within a framework of moral values that distinguishes between right and wrong. If I stay substantially within the boundaries of morality (the definition of which changes with time), I will have lived a worthwhile life.

Death is largely an unknown, but it is permanent. There may be something of me that survives after death, but it will be in a form I cannot imagine, one that will not be associated with my present consciousness or person.

If that is my paradigm and if I ask myself the questions posed at the beginning of this section as I approach my later years, I may become quite discouraged. Have I done anything to bring world peace any closer? In fact, what have I done with my life, really? Was all that time I spent working of any importance in the long run? And did I contribute anything to cooperation and love through my relationships with my family or my friends? Did I stay within the boundaries of morality as I know them? Well, it's too late to change any of that now and too late for me to do anything more about it. No wonder I may see my remaining years largely as "waiting it out."

But your self-questioning will have different results if you develop another point of view about life and its meaning. Consider this alternative paradigm:

What I call God is the Creative Force of the universe, the energy source for everything and everyone everywhere. As a human being, I am of that same energy and thus God is within me—and within everyone else. By definition, then, we are all one. We cannot truly be separated from one another, although we perceive such separateness.

The purpose of my life is to make progress in finding my soul's way back to Oneness with God. In this life I have a specific purpose to discover and fulfill. In so doing, I have lessons to learn that I have chosen before coming into this life. Whatever progress I make in that purpose and on those lessons are added to my soul's individuality, that which distinguishes my soul from the millions of other souls in similar journeys back to Oneness. I have free will and therefore may choose not to fulfill my purpose in this life. In fact, I may not even try to determine my true purpose. I may not learn the lessons I have chosen for this life, and may even go backward in my progress.

The most important principle of all is this: I create my own circumstances in life through the activity of my mind working in conjunction with my deepest motives and intents and the Creative Force of God. Actions I take in my life will be followed by reactions based on universal laws, although I may not experience those reactions in this lifetime.

This life is only one of many opportunities I have to bring myself into alignment with God, using his universal laws and the principles for living that he has presented to the world through many sources. Jesus of Nazareth was one of the individuals whom God sent into the world to provide a pattern for us. To facilitate progress toward the learning of this pattern, everyone is encouraged to develop a personal spiritual relationship with Jesus, who became the Christ.

Working from this paradigm, consider your responses to questions such as, Am I fulfilling my soul's purpose for this life? Have I learned any lessons by operating in accord with God's laws? Have I put my learning into application? In the years ahead, how may I continue to learn and apply my learning? Also, what steps can I take to prepare for my soul's next experience? Only you can answer your questions, because only you can define the issues in your life on which you have chosen to work—or choose now to work. Although the responsibility is great, so is the opportunity for movement and progress.

One intent of this book is to help you look at your future as if the latter view were your paradigm—to consider in the autumn years of this lifetime the impact of these principles and the consequences that follow from them. You may need to think more philosophically about your life and the world around you than you ever have before. You may need to come to terms with ideas and experiences that will break open the shell around your present life view so that you can grow. Making such an adjustment in your views may be as difficult as other kinds of transitions and passages people make in life, such as reported by Erikson and Levinson. In her popular book *Passages: Predictable Crises of Adult Life,* Gail Sheehy says of such adjustments:

> If we don't change, we don't grow. If we don't grow, we are not really living. Growth demands a temporary surrender of security. It may mean a giving up of familiar but limiting patterns, safe but unrewarding work, values no longer believed in, relationships that have lost their meaning.

These words aptly address the experience of changing your paradigm as you face the ambiguities of the later years.

THE OLD "NEW" IDEAS

Some of the ideas presented in the Cayce readings, such as reincarnation, seem contrary to most of Western philosophy, and especially to the Judeo-Christian tradition. Such a difference did not always exist. Some early Christian church fathers, including Justin Martyr, Clement of Alexandria, and Origen were believers in a doctrine of the "pre-existence of souls." Also, Christian Gnosticism (which included a doctrine of reincarnation) was a powerful influence on the Christian church of the first five centuries.

Then, in the year 553, the Roman Emperor Justinian, who had held Pope Vigilius prisoner for eight years, convened a special church council to ratify his "anathemas" against Origen and the doctrine of the pre-existence of the soul. Although the outcomes of that and of a subsequent council are not historically clear, they signaled the beginning of a trend in the systematic suppression of such doctrines, a trend that lasted through the Inquisition, in the thirteenth century. Then expression of belief in reincarnation became an act of heresy punishable by excommunication or even death.

Some scholars hold that segments of sacred texts that may have had more explicit references to reincarnation in Jesus's teachings were expunged or hidden from the layperson. In their extensive historical perspective titled *Reincarnation: The Phoenix Fire Mystery,* Joseph Head and S. L. Cranston ask:

> Why was the belief in reincarnation so offensive to the Defenders of the Faith? . . . [Probably because] the believer in this teaching tends to hold himself responsible for his own progress and salvation. . . . The devices (such as the confessional) of a redemption conferred by institutional authority were to believers in evolution through rebirth transparently fraudulent or false. Hence their persecution over the many centuries while dogmatic religion remained in power.

Yet there have always been courageous voices expressing these ideas, individuals whose lives reflected their commitment to acknowledging responsibility for their own circumstances. The quotations that follow are selected not to prove the idea of reincarnation, but to illustrate the diversity of people who have expressed belief in it:

Ben Franklin at seventy-nine, in a letter written in 1785, reported in *Reincarnation: The Phoenix Fire Mystery:*

> Finding myself to exist in the world, I believe I shall, in some shape or other, always exist; and, with all the inconveniences human life is liable to, I shall not object to a new edition of mine, hoping, however, that the *errata* of the last may be corrected.

Ralph Waldo Emerson at twenty-seven, in his *Journals* for 1830:

> The soul is an emanation of the Divinity, a part of the soul of the world, a ray from the source of light. It comes from without into the human body, as into a temporary abode, it goes out of it anew; it wanders in ethereal regions, it returns to visit . . . it passes into other habitations, for the soul is immortal.

Gustav Mahler at thirty-five, in 1895, as reported by Richard Specht in *Gustav Mahler:*

> We all return; it is this certainty that gives meaning to life and it does not make the slightest difference whether or not in a later incarnation we remember the former life. What counts is not the individual and his

comfort, but the great aspiration to the perfect and the pure which goes on in each incarnation.

Thomas Alva Edison at eighty, in 1927, as reported by R. F. Goudey in *Reincarnation: A Universal Truth:*

> On his eightieth birthday, Edison was asked, "Do you believe man has a soul?" He answered that man as a unit of life "is composed of swarms of billions of highly charged entities which live in the cells. I believe that when a man dies, this swarm deserts the body, and goes out into space, but keeps on and enters another cycle of life and is immortal."

Henry Ford at sixty-five, as quoted in the *San Francisco Examiner*, August 28, 1928:

> Work is futile if we cannot utilize the experience we collect in one life in the next. . . . Genius is experience. Some seem to think that it is a gift or talent, but it is the fruit of long experience in many lives. . . .
>
> If you preserve a record of this conversation, write it so that it puts men's minds at ease. I would like to communicate to others the calmness that the long view of life gives to us.

Carl Jung, at eighty-three, in 1959 in *Memories, Dreams, Reflections:*

> My life as I lived it had often seemed to me like a story that has no beginning and no end. I had the feeling that I was a historical fragment, an excerpt for which the preceding and succeeding text was missing. . . .
>
> I could well imagine that I might have lived in former centuries and there encountered questions I was not yet able to answer; that I had to be born again because I had not fulfilled the task that was given to me. When I die, my deeds will follow along with me—that is how I imagine it. I will bring with me what I have done. In the meantime it is important to insure that I do not stand at the end with empty hands.

Other views that I find meaningful are from people already in their later years who have been studying and working with the philosophy embodied in the Edgar Cayce material or parallel sources such as *A Course in Miracles*, the Unity School of Christianity, and the writings of Rudolf Steiner. I talked with a number of such people while I was writing this book, and I will quote from those conversations occasionally. Following are some of their ideas of what follows physical death and how those ideas affect their views of the elder years:

An eighty-year-old woman:

> As a result of understanding about our lives on this Earth, I find I have no fear of death. It's God's other door. It's going to be a great adventure!

A sixty-one-year-old man:

> It really doesn't matter if I'm in this body or over on the other side. I'm going to be working both places. I don't have to rush. Things are forever.

A seventy-one-year-old man:

> The Edgar Cayce readings, along with the Bible, have helped me have an increasingly strong faith in the continuity of life beyond death. Therefore I don't have any fear of death, but look upon it as God's other door opening into a new area of creative activity under God and with the help of God. This view of the creative possibilities for life after physical death gives additional, very strong impetus to one's continued creative activity right to the end.

LOOKING AHEAD WITH "NEW EYES"

The purpose of this chapter was to present a view of life different from traditional views—an alternative to stimulate new thinking about the later years. The next several chapters explore a variety of concepts, principles, and techniques that can help you be in charge of your life as you grow in wisdom and vitality as well as in years. The final two chapters can help you integrate them into your life with a plan suited to your personal interests and circumstances.

You will reap the greatest benefits from this journey with me if you accept the idea that life has a purpose beyond your conscious knowledge and motivation, and that purpose has a quality that goes beyond your conscious physical, mental, and emotional states of being. That mysterious quality has an unbreakable connection to the Universal Force that you may accept as the Creative Force, God, Infinite Wisdom, or another such concept. I will refer to the Universal Force as God. And I will use the word *spiritual*—meaning "of the spirit"—to express that aspect of life's purpose that goes beyond the physical and mental. To me, *spiritual* is not synonymous with either *religious* or *supernatural*, as they are normally defined and used.

If you are unclear or even skeptical about this spiritual connection we have with God, suspend your judgment for a while, and flow with the ideas, just to see how they fit you, how they feel to you. You have every reason to be cautious about accepting these ideas, because, as one of my eighty-year-old friends says, "The information in the Cayce readings can change the rest of your life, however long you have to live. It's never too late!"

PART II

Miles to Go

INTRODUCTION TO PART II

Miles to Go

The spirit is life; the mind is the builder; the physical is the result.

EDGAR CAYCE reading no. 349–4*

THE CAYCE READINGS FREQUENTLY remind you that, in this three-dimensional world, you have a three-dimensional consciousness. Every facet of your life can be examined from three perspectives: the spiritual, the mental, and the physical.

The spiritual perspective is centered in God—the Universal Energy, the Oneness, the Creative Force. Looking at yourself from a spiritual point of view allows you to focus on the most vital substructure of your life—the foundation on which everything else is built. Your spiritual body is the soul, and its state of development toward perfection is what Cayce calls your individuality.

---

*This is the reference number by which Edgar Cayce readings are identified. The first number represents the person receiving the reading; the second number refers to the sequence of readings for this person. This excerpt is from the fourth reading for individual number 349.

The physical perspective focuses you on the physical body you inhabit, your actions, your environment, and the events that touch your life. When you evaluate yourself from a physical point of view, you can use purely physical standards or you can adopt standards more aligned with your goals for soul development. In Cayce's terms, your personality is the sum total of how your physical body, words, and actions are seen by others.

The mental perspective is, according to the Cayce material, much more than what you ordinarily consider the mental side of consciousness—more than your awareness, your intellectual functions, and your thoughts. If you acknowledge that Spirit in its abstractness and eternal purity is at a distance from the "nowness" and potential corruptibility of the physical, you can then see the mental facet of our consciousness as the bridge, the mediator, perhaps the reconciler, between the spiritual and the physical. When you regard yourself from the mental point of view, you can assess how effective you are in connecting the perfection of Spirit to the physical circumstances in which you find yourself.

The quotation at the beginning of this introduction represents one of the most powerful principles in all the Cayce readings. The core of this idea is that the mind is the builder. This principle energizes the passive three-dimensional model into a dynamic formula for how your life is fulfilled: The mind has the capacity to draw the highest form of spiritual energy directly into your life and from that resource to build the most perfect physical results. The corollary is that the mind can also draw upon less worthy energies and produce imperfect outcomes in the physical. The wisdom to which you aspire as you grow older thus results from building your physical circumstances with elements that reinforce your inclination to draw from your richest resource: God.

The nine chapters in part II of the book offer a series of building blocks—concepts, ideas, and techniques—directed to individuals either approaching the later years of life or already experiencing them. These building blocks will enhance your individuality as well as your personality, drawing you closer to Oneness with God. In so doing, they will give new meaning to your later years.

These building blocks all have a mental quality, because they involve your mind as you put them to use in your life. They are presented, however, according to whether they emphasize the *spiritual* connection with God, concentrate on traditional *mental* functions, or focus on *physical* circumstances. Chapters 3 through 5 deal with the building blocks of the spirit, chapters 6 through 8 with those of the mind, and chapters 9 through 11 with those of the body.

3

Life Ideals and Mission:
The Purpose of It All

*First analyze self, self's ideals, self's purpose. Know thy
ideal in spiritual, in mental, in material things.*
EDGAR CAYCE reading no. 3091–1

THOSE FIRST HEARING ABOUT having an ideal and a mission in
life at age sixty, might respond with a discouraged "*Now* you tell
me!" The time when something could be done about a mission may
seem to be behind them. Ahead of them may seem to be few opportunities for progressing toward a newly expressed purpose in life.

Not so! For a start, the preceding reading was given for a seventy-
two-year-old woman on whom Cayce's source was trying to impress
that it's never too late. If the soul's individuality continues beyond
physical death, steps toward spiritual growth are appropriate at any
age.

In *The Seasons of a Man's Life*, Daniel Levinson suggests that the
later years are probably the best time to get your priorities straight,
to follow your vision of purpose and meaning:

> After "retirement" [from formal employment] he can engage in valued
> work, but it now stems more from his own creative energies than from

external pressure and financial need. Having paid his dues to society, he has earned the right to be and do what is most important to himself.

The words "valued work . . . creative energies . . . to be and do what is most important to himself" could well relate to the task of discovering and working with your mission and ideals. So it is quite timely to identify your life ideals and mission at this stage of life. Not that the task should be saved until this period in life, but conditions are excellent if you haven't done it before now. If you have, the time is right for reviewing earlier formulations from the vantage point of your present age and circumstances.

The very activity of seeking the purpose for your life helps to satisfy an apparently innate need humans have to find a pattern to the many threads of life and to recognize a wholeness—an integrity, in Erikson's terms—in that pattern. In *Vital Involvement in Old Age*, Erikson says,

> Today's elder must reface issues of identity and identity confusion by seeking to integrate current caring, love, faithfulness, competence, purposefulness, willfulness, and hopefulness in contemporary society with earlier-life values, beliefs, and commitments. This final integration is essential to old age's consolidation of a lifelong sense of oneself.

In *Oh, to Be Fifty Again!* Eda LeShan broadly echoes this sentiment:

> The search for meaning, for seeing our lives as useful and purposeful . . . is a fundamental necessity all through life, but never more significant than when we begin to get old.

DISCOVERING YOUR LIFE'S IDEALS

The Edgar Cayce readings give high priority to work with ideals, going so far as to say that "the most important experience of this or any individual . . . is to first know what IS the ideal—spiritually" (no. 357–13).

When you use the word *ideal* in everyday conversation, you usually mean something that represents a standard of perfection, a model to emulate. Paralleling the traditional use of the word, the readings refer to the ideal as "something to look up to, or to attempt to attain to." The readings go further by suggesting that you should strive toward the ideal and may even experience a portion of it, but cannot achieve it completely. The fact that its complete and perfect achievement is beyond you should not dismay you, but instead help you realize which of your aims or standards is truly an ideal rather than merely a goal or objective.

Levinson's interviews and observations of the men in his study reported in *The Seasons of a Man's Life* led to his concept of the Dream. In the following excerpts, if the word *ideal* is substituted for *Dream*, the statements illustrate many of the same qualities as Cayce's concept of *ideal:*

> The Dream . . . has the quality of a vision, an imagined possibility that generates excitement and vitality.
>
> If the Dream remains unconnected to his life, it may simply die, and with it his sense of aliveness and purpose.
>
> The Dream may be modest or heroic, vaguely defined or crystal clear, a burning passion or a quiet guiding force, a source of inspiration, strength and corrosive conflict. Some men make the pursuit of the Dream the central element in the life structure and build everything else around it.
>
> My life is enriched to the extent that I have a Dream and give it an appropriate place in my life. . . . If I have no Dream or can find no way to live it out, my life lacks genuine purpose or meaning.

In keeping with the lawful sequence that the spirit is life, the mind is the builder, and the physical is the result, the fundamental ideal is a spiritual ideal, which has counterparts in mental and physical ideals. Your task as an individual seeker is to identify first the spiritual ideal that undergirds your life, moves you to the highest human motives, and stimulates the best that is in you. Once you know your spiritual ideal, you can bring it into your day-to-day life by applying the mental and physical ideals through which it manifests.

You already have a spiritual ideal, hidden or ignored though it may be. You have only to identify it and acknowledge its impact on your life. You are then able to derive mental and physical ideals consistent with your spiritual ideal, and use them as standards against which to measure your thoughts and actions, adjusting behavior that does not measure up.

To the degree that you conduct your life in a manner consistent with your ideals, you align yourself with your ultimate spiritual purpose, and you have access to the infinite resources of God. When you act against those ideals, you encounter barriers, lacks, and confusion in your life, and your resources appear limited. The ideals are so critical to your life that Cayce's readings say, "What we are . . . is the combined result of what we have done about the ideals that we have set!" (no. 1549–1).

In the "new eyes" view of the spiritual path, a return to Oneness with God is your ultimate destiny. Thus Oneness with God is everyone's ultimate spiritual ideal. If I try to use that ideal as a standard against which to check my thoughts and actions, however, I may find Oneness with God too abstract for such an evaluation. Instead, I try to identify a more tangible ideal consistent with Oneness, a working-level concept that seems to be a strong motivator in my life and with which I can find closer identification. Examples include loving service, peace and harmony, unconditional love, faith, and patience. Because spiritual development progresses differently for different people, you can expect the expression of your ideals to differ according to the issues on which you have chosen to focus.

You may have as personal heroes individuals whose lives and work represent the influence of their spiritual ideal. For me, Hubert Humphrey represents an individual who brought to the field of politics and government service a set of values and ideals that conveyed the best of what we might be. Hubert Humphrey is quoted as saying, in Carl Solberg's *Hubert Humphrey: A Biography*,

> I have always believed that freedom was possible. I have always believed that the basic decency within this nation would one day enable us to lift the veil from our eyes and see each other for what we are as people—not black or white, not rich or poor, not attending one church or another—but as people standing equally together, free of hate or suspicion.

A statement like that suggests that Humphrey operated as though his working spiritual ideal was human freedom and equality. The people we most admire often have ideals similar to our own.

In *Where I Lived and What I Lived For*, Henry David Thoreau expresses a concept akin to the spiritual ideal:

> We must learn to reawaken and keep ourselves awake . . . by an infinite expectation of the dawn. . . . I know of no more encouraging fact than the unquestionable ability of man to elevate his life by a conscious endeavor. . . . Every man is tasked to make his life . . . worthy of the contemplation of his most elevated and critical hour.

Taking a cue from Thoreau, you can use the contemplation of your most elevated hours as a means of discovering your own spiritual ideal.

GETTING PERSONAL

Your spiritual ideal is having an effect on your life every day, even if you have never expressed it in your conscious mind. Your task is to identify some of the influences your ideal has had in your life and to deduce from the results what the ideal is.

Below are six activities to help you identify your life ideal. Use your journal or notebook to write your responses to each query:

1. List three individuals whom you greatly admire and respect because of their actions or stated principles. They may or may not be living now. They may be well-known personalities, little-known people, relatives, friends, or acquaintances.

2. List one or more personal qualities each of these three individuals represents to you, or an accomplishment of each that you admire.

3. Think back over your own life and work, especially your recent years. Select one or more actions, accomplishments, or ongoing activities that have given you a long-lasting good

feeling about yourself. Can you think of a moment in time when you felt exhilaration, a taste of divine ecstasy, a sense of being at one with the world? What brought about that moment?

4. Assume you are being introduced at a large banquet at which you will receive an award. What are some of your qualities, talents, accomplishments, or strengths you would be especially pleased to have the introducer mention?

5. Review what you have written so far in this exercise. Try to find common elements or a pattern in what you value highly in others and in yourself. As if you were describing someone else, write a brief summary that integrates these elements. For example:

   He writes and speaks well, is articulate in expressing his opinions and ideas. He stands up for what he believes in, such as his deep concern for the less able, less fortunate, and the wronged or abused.

6. Given what you already knew about yourself, amplified by what you may have discovered in this exercise, write down a word or phrase that appears to be an underlying motivator for your life. Consider this your first formulation of your working spiritual ideal. You can always adjust it later as you work with it and test it in your life. For example, the working spiritual ideal for the description in step 5 above might be "service to those who cannot help themselves."

———————————————

So far I have concentrated on the spiritual ideal, which is the key to your motivation. In keeping with the three-dimensional environment of your life, its influence will be felt through its application in the mental and physical aspects of your life. And as your life changes, the ways in which your spiritual ideal expresses itself mentally and physically will also change, even though the spiritual ideal itself does not change.

Consider mental and physical ideals in the following way. Mental ideals relate to your attitudes, emotions, thoughts, and plans. For example, let's say my spiritual ideal is peace and harmony in the world. One of my mental ideals might be to look for agreements and similarities in what I read and hear, rather than conflicts and differences. Another mental ideal might be to give higher priority to reading or viewing articles, books, and TV programs related to peace and nonviolence. Physical ideals relate to your actions, words, and physical expressions. From the spiritual ideal of peace and harmony, one physical ideal might be to commend others for agreements and peaceful actions; another might be to write letters to sponsors of TV programs highlighting violence and the glorification of war, suggesting they support more peaceful, nonviolent programming.

Remember that an ideal is like a yardstick in your life: it can be used to measure your thoughts, actions, and anticipated actions. When you state your ideals in a form you can readily relate to, it will be easier to use them as criteria for your day-to-day thoughts and actions.

GETTING PERSONAL

One way to help your ideals permeate your life is to write them separately for several areas of your life. Table 3 provides space at the top for you to write your working spiritual ideal from the preceding exercise, so that you keep focused on that ideal. The rest of the worksheet is divided horizontally into different areas of your life: your self, your significant relationships, and your principal activities.

Under "Self," develop both a mental and a physical ideal for the spiritual side of your life, another pair of ideals for your mental side, and a third pair for your physical side.

For example, a mental ideal for the spiritual side might be to schedule at least a half hour every day for activities designed to add to your spiritual development, such as reading spiritual growth books. A physical ideal for the spiritual side of your life might be to attend each month at least one program or event with a spiritual theme.

Table 3
Worksheet on Life Ideals

Ultimate spiritual ideal: Oneness with God
My working spiritual ideal (from preceding exercise):

AREAS OF LIFE	MENTAL IDEALS Attitudes, thoughts, emotions, ideas, plans	PHYSICAL IDEALS Actions, activities, words, accomplishments
Self: Spiritual self		
Mental self		
Physical self		
Relationships: ——————— ——————— ———————		

Table 3
Worksheet on Life Ideals (continued)

AREAS OF LIFE	MENTAL IDEALS Attitudes, thoughts, emotions, ideas, plans	PHYSICAL IDEALS Actions, activities, words, accomplishments
Primary activities or settings: _____ _____ _____		

Under "Relationships," write the names of as many as three people with whom you have significant relationships (family, friends, work colleagues, or recreation partners). Then for each of them, develop a mental and a physical ideal.

Under "Primary activities or settings," write as many as three activities or settings that are significant in your life, such as your home, volunteer activity, place of employment, place of worship, regular card-playing group, and so on. Then for each of them, develop a mental and a physical ideal.

APPLYING YOUR IDEALS

Many of the chapters that follow refer to your ideal in some specific application. Perhaps the most important application is in your day-to-day activity, using the ideal as a standard for what you say and do. An illustration of this application process will help you to understand it:

Let's continue with the example that my spiritual ideal is universal peace, with a more specific ideal of peace and harmony in the world I touch. Samples of my mental and physical ideals were presented earlier.

Assume I find myself in a group of friends who begin to argue about whether women are discriminated against in employment—the jobs they get, the pay they receive, the atmosphere in which they work. Assume further that I have strong feelings about the issue and would enjoy a lively argument with anyone who believes the days of discrimination against women are over.

My inclination without considering ideals is to jump in to convince others to take my point of view. Applying my ideals, however, I approach this situation differently. I don't walk away because that would not serve the cause of peace. Instead I try to find ways to keep the discussion at a rational level, even looking for points I can endorse on the side of "no more discrimination"—"You're certainly right when you say more women than ever before are in top management jobs" or "It's true that the take-home pay for many women has gone up in the past ten years." I may also try to keep my fellow supporters of "discrimination still exists" from being argumentative or even insulting—"Come on now, friend. Let's talk about specific experiences we know about" or "I think you'll make your point better if you stay away from words like that."

Because my ideals relate to peace, I am especially aware of situations and actions with potential conflict, and I approach them conscious of the need to use my ideals as my standard of behavior.

Measuring every anticipated action or word against your ideal does not seem practical. Yet once your ideal has been internalized, the effect is just that. To reach that internalization, the Cayce readings suggest at least two kinds of self-discipline:

The prospective approach: Pick an hour or a day ahead of you, or an upcoming event, such as a meeting or a social event, and plan to focus on your ideals during that period. You might find it helpful to wear or carry something to remind you about it periodically; you might, for example, wear a ring on a different finger, or your watch on the opposite wrist. Approach individuals and situations during that period with the intent of putting your ideal into action.

The *retrospective* approach: At the end of the day, think back over the events of the day with your ideal in mind. Were there situations in which you might have acted or spoken more in accord with your ideals? The purpose is not to chastise yourself, but to alert yourself to the kinds of situations you encounter where you can use your ideals to help you cope more effectively.

Do not expect to become perfect in your application of ideals. Take heart from the Cayce readings that say, for example, "It is the 'try' that is more often counted as righteousness, and *not* the success or failure" (no. 931–1).

DISCOVERING YOUR LIFE'S PURPOSE OR MISSION

Just as every soul has as its ultimate ideal Oneness with God, every soul has as its ultimate purpose or mission the preparations for that Oneness. The Cayce readings use phrases such as these: to "become more aware or conscious of the Divine within" (no. 518–2), to "manifest to the glory of God and to the honor of self" (no. 3333–1), and to "be as a light unto others" (no. 641–6).

From the ultimate spiritual ideal, you have just developed a first estimate of what a working ideal is—one you can relate to on a daily basis. Similarly, you can develop a first conception of your life's mission—one for which you can set your goals and plan your priorities. "For, each soul enters with a mission. . . . We all have a mission to perform" (no. 3003–1).

How will you know if you have discovered your life's mission? Cayce's readings suggest that when your thoughts and actions are aligned with your life ideals and purposes, you will experience these signs, as summarized in Mark Thurston's *Discovering Your Soul's Purpose*:

1. a sense of expanding awareness that brings with it the feeling of wonder and awe about life;
2. a feeling of closeness to others that comes from having given to them without expecting something in return;
3. a sense of greater wholeness, of being more complete, of being closer to God;

4. a deeper insight into how all of life is purposeful; and
5. a feeling of great joy.

Is it worth trying to discover your soul's purpose at this stage of your life? Perhaps it is more relevant to ask, Would you like to experience more of the emotions just named in your life? Remember that the Cayce reading at the opening of this chapter was given for a seventy-two-year-old woman. A similar instruction was given to a seventy-nine-year-old man, one of the oldest people receiving readings (no. 3189–2).

To make the idea of mission more tangible, here are some examples of mission themes identified by people working with the Cayce concepts on the soul's purpose:

> to work for justice
> to be a spokesperson for truth
> to be a transmitter and clarifier of ideas
> to be a catalyst for change
> to serve others in humbleness
> to be an agent of inner and outer peace
> to bring hope to others
> to bring things to completion
> to cooperate with Spirit in nature
> to manifest God's love through the family

As someone approaching or in the later years, you have perhaps a greater insight into your strengths and aptitudes than a younger person has. What follows is an exercise to help you use your special vantage point to develop a hypothesis about your soul's mission in this life. The exercise that follows parallels Mark Thurston's approach.

GETTING PERSONAL

Write the responses to the following self-analysis items in your notebook or journal. Your notes and responses from the preceding exercise on ideals will be useful.

1. Think about each of these four periods in your life:

    Childhood and adolescence (to age twenty or so)
    Early adulthood (from about twenty to about thirty-five)
    Middle adulthood (from about thirty-five to about fifty)
    Late middle adulthood (from about fifty on)

    For each period briefly write notes about one experience that gave you moments when you had some of these feelings:

    feeling more complete as a person
    experiencing the wonder of life and living
    feeling a heightened awareness of everything around you
    experiencing great joy
    feeling, This is really me!
    feeling closer to someone after giving unselfishly of
        yourself
    seeing purposefulness in life around you
    feeling closer to God, sensing the presence of God

    For the experience you select in each life period, write down what you were doing and the feelings you remember. What do you think gave you these feelings? Is there any theme common to what you were doing that gave rise to these feelings?

2. Now make a list of your strengths and talents. Include those you use regularly and also those you have not had much opportunity to exercise. (You may have some useful notes from the preceding exercise on ideals.)

3. Look over your list from number 2. Do any of your strengths or talents ever cause you surprise? Do any cause you to feel, Now where did *that* come from? Are there any where learning came so easily that it hardly took conscious effort? Put a checkmark beside those that meet these tests.

4. Review the experiences you described in number 1 and review the list from number 2. Did any of the listed abilities play a role in any of your selected experiences? Put a star beside those that did. When you are working with any of these

abilities, do you ever have some of the feelings listed in number 1? Put a star beside those also.

5. Finally, focusing on the listed items that you checked or starred, select three or four strengths or talents that seem to cluster together. Can you see a pattern that suggests a life mission? Try to write a phrase that represents your first formulation of your mission based on these key characteristics.

> For example, assume I picked these from my list: imagination, teaching, writing, and helping others use their capabilities. One version of a mission statement might be this: My mission is to help others, through my creative teaching and writing, to use their own abilities.

You may not be able to express all of your key strengths in the statement, but could use them all in carrying out the mission.

——————————————

Once you have a tentative statement about your life's mission, you can begin to test its validity. Only by trying out the mission can you discover whether it is right for you. When you take your first steps to carry out that mission, you will detect signals around you that either confirm or deny your direction and purpose.

For example, starting with the mission statement, "My mission is to help others, through my creative teaching and writing, to use their own abilities," I would first create an opportunity for testing. Let's say I decided to talk to my church pastor about writing an article and questionnaire for the church newsletter encouraging church members to participate in small group meetings where they could share their experiences and abilities with others having similar interests. Confirming signals would include enthusiasm on the part of the pastor, available space in the newsletter, a good response from the church members, and, finally, of course, actual meetings taking place with lots of sharing and enthusiasm among participants. Denial signals would include opposite reactions or negative experiences.

Obviously a single successful test does not confirm the mission statement, but it is a start. You follow up with other activities and projects designed to further your mission, watching the signs around you as you plan and carry them out. After two or three such projects, you will have a strong sense of whether or not your mission is appropriately stated. You may want to revise your wording of the mission, or go even further back in your preparatory work to change your selection of strengths or talents, for example, before restating the mission itself. Through such a trial-and-error process, you will eventually have confidence in what you have identified as your soul's purpose or mission.

If your mission seems overwhelmingly ambitious to you, keep in mind Cayce's frequent reminder: "Start where you are, that all may be perfectly understood! For it is line upon line, precept upon precept [that] we grow in grace, in knowledge, in understanding" (no. 349–1).

4

Meditation and Prayer: Communicating Where It Counts

Prayer is supplication to God and meditation is listening to His answer.
EDGAR CAYCE reading no. 2946–6

How OFTEN HAVE YOU heard someone say that communication was at the heart of some misunderstanding or impasse—whether between the president and Congress, between worker and boss, between wife and husband, or between parent and child? Relationships prosper when the parties talk openly, honestly, and completely; they deteriorate when communication is guarded, infrequent, untruthful, or incomplete.

The principles that guide good communication with other people are equally valid when you communicate with God. The infinite resources available to you through God are limited only by your unwillingness or inability to communicate with God.

How do you know when God is ready to communicate with you, willing to give you guidance? Readiness and willingness imply periods when God is not available, a source that responds only selectively. The Cayce readings frequently refer to the following verses from Jesus' Sermon on the Mount:

> Ask, and it will be given you; seek, and you will find; knock, and it will be opened to you. For every one who asks receives, and he who seeks finds, and to him who knocks it will be opened. (Matt. 7:7–8)

If the Creative Forces are always available to you and you have only to request them, why do you continue in need, especially in your later years? Two possible reasons are that you do not feel you deserve God's help as much as someone else does (as if there were limits on the supply), or you are not sure how to go about asking for God's help (as if God expected you to observe specific rituals or rules of protocol).

As to your worthiness of God's help, when you grow older you may begin to settle for less and less of what life has to offer. You may say to yourself, "After all, I had my chance. Now that my productive years are over, it's time to step into the background." So you may find yourself backing down from relationships, settling for less communication, feeling in some way that the events of your life and the problems you face do not matter as much as do those of younger people. In so doing, your lesser communication can foster retreat, isolation, and unnecessary limits on your life.

This reduced communication level may affect your relationship with God as well as your relationships with those around you. You may thank God for the many blessings you have had, but you may feel that what remains of your life is not worth troubling God about.

Then, too, might you be apprehensive about the potential that still remains for you if you try for more in life?

Another biblical passage that Edgar Cayce frequently quoted addresses this kind of resigned attitude:

> I have set before you life and death, . . . therefore choose life, . . . loving the Lord your God, . . . for that means life to you. (Deut. 30:19–20)

"Choose life!" What a banner, especially if you feel there is little to expect in the latter part of your life! And when you choose life by showing your love for God through your actions as well as your communications, you can tap into those resources of God that will make life worth living. To do so, however, you must address the second reason why you lack: you are not sure how to reach God and ask for the help you would like. Recognizing that the older you are, the more questions you may have to ask God, what better time than now to refresh your conversational skills?

BECOMING CONVERSATIONALISTS WITH GOD

You no doubt accepted responsibility for maintaining communication with your earthly parents, even if irregularly. But perhaps you have not kept up your end of the communication link with God—not because you don't believe in God, but because you assume that an omniscient, omnipresent God knows your needs and concerns, whether you consciously address them to him or not: "God is always present and knows what I think and do, so why should I need to express myself to God in words?"

The Cayce readings recognize the human tendency to view God in at least two contrasting ways: as God the impersonal force everywhere present in the universe, and as God the intelligent, listening mind always available to every individual on Earth, always aware of each persons' individual needs and how to meet them. What you may forget is that God also created you with free will, which puts the responsibility squarely on you to shape your own destiny—and that includes the responsibility to ask for God's help when you need it, instead of assuming help will come unbidden. Jesus was clear about this in the passage quoted earlier: *ask* and it will be given, *seek* and you will find, *knock* and the door will be opened.

Once you choose to talk with God, you take steps to make your communication link as clear as possible by attuning your consciousness to God. Meditation is the process for such attunement, and prayer is the language for your communication.

A few spiritual leaders appear to maintain a state of almost continuous attunement with God. Such individuals apparently spend much of their time in meditation and prayer even as they go about their worldly business. You might not aspire to such a state of enlightenment, but you can facilitate your own attunement with God through regular meditation. Practice may not make it perfect, but it will result in a clearer, more accessible channel to God at all times.

It may sound like you cannot talk to God without attuning yourself to him through meditation. Of course, that's not so. You can always communicate with God, with or without meditating. If a car headed in your direction hurtles across the median strip, you do not have time to meditate before calling for God's help. Because you have free will, however, you must ask for help, even in such a crisis.

Regular meditation and prayer provide additional opportunities for you to grow spiritually. A Cayce reading says,

> Don't let a day go by without meditation and prayer for some definite purpose, and not for self, but that self may be the channel of help to someone else. For in helping others is the greater way to help self. (no. 3624–1)

In summary, you have a God-given communication channel to the Creative Forces of the universe, but you also have the God-given free will that makes you individually responsible for opening that channel, tuning in to God, and initiating the communication. The attunement is facilitated by meditation, just as the communication is facilitated by prayer. Meditation and prayer should be frequent, so that you can become more experienced in your communicating and so that you can have daily opportunities to serve others through your prayers.

AFFIRMATIONS—POWER IN SMALL PACKAGES

I'll begin an exploration of prayer and meditation with one of the simplest, most versatile, and most useful tools for communicating with God—the affirmation.

Because your spiritual ideal is aligned with God's purpose for you—Oneness—that ideal is a strong tool for attuning yourself with God. Therefore, one aid in the attunement process is to maintain a focus on your ideals through affirmations—positive statements you express about a spiritual truth. As an affirmation is repeated with earnestness and accepted with faith, the truth within it begins to follow the path from spirit to mind to body. You start to bring into physical manifestation the outcome of that affirmative process.

A series of 130 Cayce readings given over a period of eleven years provides a step-by-step approach to spiritual development through small-group activity. For each lesson in these readings on *A Search for God*, the Cayce source provides at least one affirmation. Many of these are extended affirmations that include elements of prayer. For example, in the lesson on righteousness, this affirmation is given:

> Create in me, O God, a new purpose, a righteous spirit: That I may, as Thy child, be a living example of that I have professed and do profess to believe, by manifesting same among my fellow men. (no. 262–124)

Many of these instructional affirmations contain phrases and short statements that can be used as simple affirmations in your own prayer and meditation. Some examples:

> Not my will but Thine, O Lord (no. 262–3).
>
> Make us more aware of *God is Love* (no. 262–43).
>
> Let me—my mind, my body, my soul—be at one with Thee (no. 262–88).

Because such phrases reflect the common spiritual purpose of all humanity, such affirmations may be adopted by anyone on the spiritual journey. You will find, however, special meaning in affirmations you create from your own spiritual, mental, and physical ideals, stated in your own words and tailored to your own circumstances.

Meaningful personal affirmations can also be invaluable mini-prayers quickly recalled in urgent life situations. One of my elder conversation partners, who meditates regularly, described a situation that illustrates this:

> While lifting some luggage on a trip, something slipped in my lower back, and the pain knocked me off my feet. As I lay on my back, I immediately began repeating an affirmation that everything was in divine order. That got me into a kind of meditation state and started the healing process right away. In a few minutes I was able to get up and move

well enough to finish the trip before getting an adjustment to my back. Affirmations are lifesavers for me in a lot of situations.

So that you can take advantage of this powerful tool, here's an opportunity to create two affirmations of your own.

GETTING PERSONAL

You will first create an affirmation that contains the essence of your spiritual ideal. This will be used as a focus in your meditation exercise later in this chapter.

Consider your spiritual ideal, as expressed during the exercises in Chapter 3. Develop a short sentence or phrase that incorporates the essence of that ideal.

For example, for an ideal of loving service, the affirmation might be, "I serve with love," or, in a lighter tone and with a rhythm, "I love to serve, and serve with love."

For ideals related to peace, affirmations might be, "Peace begins with me," "Peace is within and around me," "Where I go, peace follows," or "Peace leads me on and I follow."

The idea is to represent in the short statement the central theme of your ideal and how it relates to you and your actions. Select words and phrases that are comfortable for you, and put them together in a way that has the most meaning for you and that can readily be remembered. You may want to select and arrange the words so that the affirmation has a natural rhythm or cadence to it.

Another kind of affirmation is specific to an issue in your life that you frequently deal with, perhaps even on a daily basis.

For example, I have chronic tendonitis in one wrist that causes discomfort after extended physical activity. I can try to ignore it, or I can take pain-killing medication, or I can use an affirmation for both physical and mental healing: "I accept this pain as a reminder of a physical limitation. I now release it as healing takes place." The words may not always be the same, but they include acknowledgment of the pain, followed by release, while affirming healing. I can use this affirmation no matter where I am or what I am doing, and it attunes me quickly with God's healing energy.

Select an issue on which you would like help in controlling your actions or reactions. If it's a physical problem, you can adapt the preceding example to your own needs, or you can create an affirmation wholly your own. Difficulties in interpersonal relationships can also be eased through affirmations.

As an example, when I encounter a man with whom I am at odds, I might affirm, "We are both children of God and therefore brothers under the skin," or "Lord, he is yours and I am yours. Let your will be done," or "I release all differences and feelings of negativity to God—right now." Such affirmations help remind me of our common relationship with God, and lend a perspective that shows our disagreements to be trivial.

Take time now to select an issue you can use help on, and create an affirmation to reduce the negative effects of that issue. Select words and phrases you are comfortable with, and create an affirmation you will be able to remember.

————————————

PRAYER—TALKING TO GOD

Because you will be incorporating prayer into the meditation process, you will first consider the language and structure of prayer, and then you will prepare prayers for use in meditation.

Asking for help is not the only form of prayer, probably not even the most frequent. I discuss requests for help and also six other types of prayer in the following paragraphs. One prayer often incorporates several types of prayer within it.

Praise: You probably assumed your earthly parents or others who took care of you knew you loved them even if you did not tell them so. Yet a spontaneous, sincere expression of your love and appreciation touched something in them not reachable by any other action. So it is with your expressions to God. Prayers of praise help to remind you of God's infinite love for you, and they communicate to God your love and sense of awe: "Our Father who art in heaven, hallowed be thy name"; "Praise God from whom all blessings flow"; "I love you, Father/Mother God."

Thanksgiving: One woman I know starts her days with the prayer, "This is the day the Lord has made. Let us give thanks and be glad." Joyful thanksgiving should be a significant part of your communication with God. Do you say, "Thank you, God" following positive events? One man I know believes spiritual development takes giant steps forward when you can say, "Thank you, God" for everything that happens, "good or bad," because "nothing is truly bad": "Thank you, Father, for all my years"; "Thank you, God, for all the blessings you have given to me and my family."

Trust and faith: Did you ever say to someone you trusted, "I'll do whatever you think is best"? Have you said that to God lately? You have if you've recited The Lord's Prayer: "Thy will be done." When I desire something, I still want to be consistent with God's purpose, so I use a phrase from the first of the Cayce Search for God affirmations: "Not my will, but Thine, O Lord." In contrast to experiences where you must express your own free will, this type of prayer represents a kind of humility, expressing the sincere desire that your self-serving motives be transformed into God-serving purposes: "If it's your will, Father, help me to continue living independently in my home."

Protection: Before meditation: "As I open myself to unseen forces, I surround myself with the protection of God's love." Before entering a potentially difficult interpersonal situation: "I place around myself the white light of God's protection." And before traveling: "God, keep us safe and healthy on our trip."

Personal request: This is sometimes referred to as a petition; you are asking for something for yourself. You might be tempted to word a request as if you knew what was right for you, and could therefore choose the best course for yourself: "God, please help me to get the money together to purchase a new car." In fact, you may be limiting yourself by asking only for those things you see as possibilities. As I mentioned under trust and faith, coupling such a petition with trust results in statements such as, "As I enter this situation, help me to know your will and to act as you would have me do" or, "Help me, God, to select the living arrangement that will be in accord with your will."

Forgiveness: This gives you a chance to say you want to be forgiven, by others as well as by God, for your inappropriate thoughts, words, or actions or failures to act: "Please forgive me, God, for being so judgmental about Sue this morning, and help Sue to forgive me too." You can also seek God's help in forgiving others: "Help me, Lord, to forgive Pat's actions toward me." The Lord's Prayer states, "Forgive us our trespasses as we forgive those who trespass against us." Do you really forgive others as readily as you would like to be forgiven? As an elder, you may get a lot of opportunities to be forgiving if you think others are ignoring you, taking advantage of you, or demeaning you in some way. Your prayers of forgiveness help to dissolve resentments: "I forgive them, Father, as you do."

Request for others: It is fine to be a channel for others in your prayers and meditation, but recognize that you are limited in understanding your own needs, and even less likely to understand the needs of someone else. So be cautious in your use of intercessory prayer, as it is sometimes called. In answer to the question, "How do you know when to help an individual?" a Cayce reading answered:

> Do with thy might what thine hands, hearts, minds, souls, find to do, leaving the increase, the benefits, in *His* hands, who is the Giver of all good and perfect gifts. (no. 281–4)

That suggests that your prayers for others should leave the solutions and benefits for God to choose: "O God, please send your light and love to Charlie Jones, providing him with what you know best for him" or, "Please surround Betsy Smith with the light of your love."

Here is a sample prayer that incorporates all of the types of prayer I have discussed:

> O God of infinite wisdom and love, I love you more deeply every day (praise). I am thankful for the many blessings of my life (thanksgiving). Please help me to know how I can reduce the limitations my current physical ailments are imposing on me (personal request). Please forgive

me my impatience with my ailments (forgiveness). Give me insight into my relationships with my children (personal request). Surround them and their children in your light and love (request for others), and keep them safe on their journey (protection). Help me always to know and to do Thy will (trust and faith). Amen.

If you review The Lord's Prayer phrase by phrase, you will identify five of the seven types of prayers starting and ending with praise, and including trust and faith, personal request, forgiveness, and protection.

GETTING PERSONAL

Review each of the seven prayer types and how each of them might relate to something in your life right now. Then write a prayer of several sentences as the basis for a meaningful communication with God. Divide the prayer into two parts, concentrating on praise, thanksgiving, trust and faith, and protection in the first part, to be used at the beginning of meditation. The second part will include personal requests, prayers of forgiveness, and requests for others, to be offered after attunement.

MEDITATION—LISTENING TO GOD

Many who received readings from Edgar Cayce were urged to "enter into the holy of holies within the self, where the promise has been ever that there thy Lord may meet thee" (no. 657–3). Whether your state of mind is fear, confusion, doubt, or desire, you may always seek God within you through the meditative experience.

Many scientific studies have demonstrated that meditation can produce beneficial effects both physiologically and psychologically for people in a wide range of ages and circumstances. For example, research on meditation among older people suggests that some forms of meditation may improve the mental skills of elders as well as increase their longevity. As reported in the American Psychological Association's *Monitor* in October 1986, a three-year study of seventy-three residents in homes for the elderly (average age eighty-one) by Harvard psychologists Charles Alexander and Ellen Langer found that the regular practice of transcendental meditation (TM) resulted not only in improved performance in several mental and physical areas, but also in apparent increases in longevity among these residents. This finding is consistent with earlier studies published in 1982 in the *International Journal of Neuroscience* by Keith Wallace, a neurophysiologist who found that long-term TM meditators appeared biologically younger than short-term meditators, who in turn appeared biologically younger than nonmeditators.

Reporting on their study to the National Council on the Aging, Charles Alexander expressed the view that meditation that includes both a state of relaxation and a state of alertness (as TM does) can result in greater empowerment for those in their later years—empowerment characterized by less dependency on outside forms of support, a greater ability to participate in decisions, and ultimately a greater control of their own lives. "Directly transforming one's state of consciousness [through regular meditation]," said Alexander, "can cause a change in mind and body that translates literally into the extension of human life and enhancement of the quality of life."

In *Oh, to Be Fifty Again!* Eda LeShan suggests other reasons for working with meditation and prayer in the later years:

> The value of introspection, meditation, or prayer is not only that it can help in the process of self-discovery, but that beyond that it may help us to have the courage to be innovators at a time in our lives when we may be retiring from the work we've been doing for a long time, when we may need new interests and sources of inner gratification, and when we may very possibly have to be quite resourceful about finding new ways of earning money.

And later LeShan adds

> Older people need meditation as a way of cultivating the special developmental task at hand—to begin to move from a focus on the material world to the larger world of the human spirit.

A summary of some of the research on the benefits of meditation appears at the end of Mark Thurston's *Inner Power of Silence: A Universal Way of Meditation.* But none of the studies addresses the contribution made to meditation by a spiritual component—the concept of alignment with God, for example. Science may never develop a satisfactory technology to do so. Does a spiritual focus in meditation further enhance the mental and physical benefits demonstrated without such a focus? More important, does the spiritual focus facilitate spiritually oriented outcomes—increased awareness that you are a spiritual being, demonstration of spiritual principles in your life, movement toward Oneness with God? From the results of research involving members of the Association for Research and Enlightenment—A.R.E., the organization founded by Edgar Cayce in 1931—you can be certain that many experienced meditators would answer with a resounding yes to such questions.

Regardless of the form in which you prefer your evidence—the Cayce readings themselves, scientific research results, or reports of meditators—there's a strong case for meditating in your later years, even if you have never meditated before.

The Cayce readings describe meditation in different ways to different people. They acknowledge that meditation is a personal activity and must accommodate the individual's experience, living circumstances, and state of spiritual development. Each person should of his or her "own volition and desire perfect that approach which to the self answers that need within" (no. 2441–2). No one can tell you exactly how to meditate, Cayce continues, any more than "one may tell another how to fall in love" (no. 2441–2).

The suggestions that follow are fundamentals derived from a great many Cayce readings concerning meditation. They are presented here in three stages: preparation, attunement, and application.

Stage One: Preparing for Meditation

Preparing for meditation is a refinement of the kinds of preparations you might make for an important communication with another person: you establish a setting and an attitude where you can concentrate on what you are doing, where you can talk seriously and calmly, and where you can listen without distraction to what the other person is saying. Prior to entering the attunement stage of meditation, you should make several physical and mental preparations:

Pick a time that will allow you to meditate at about the same hour every day. Many meditators find a period early in the day most convenient and least likely to be disrupted by other activities. Getting up at a regular time for meditation can also help you maintain a daily schedule for other activities. Also, what better time for an attunement with the universe than soon after awaking from sleep, before meeting the challenges of the day? But choose any time suited to your daily schedule.

One of the older people I spoke with confirmed from experience Cayce's emphasis on regularity of meditation: "Don't let a day go by. . . ." She said that when she allowed other activities to interfere with her meditation, she was more inclined to feel scattered during the day. Then too she felt she had "nothing to fall back on"—no reserve supply of strength and energy to carry her through the challenges of the day. This sentiment is echoed by many who meditate regularly.

When you first start the practice of meditating, the length of the meditation period may be only a few minutes. It is better to spend only five minutes every day than fifteen minutes two or three times a week. And when your meditations are longer, it is preferable to meditate even five minutes on a day when your schedule won't allow more time than to skip meditation that day. The regularity and consistency of meditating appear to be more important than the total amount of time spent. I personally find fifteen to twenty minutes first thing in the morning a comfortable, helpful meditation period.

The Cayce readings recommend that you purify your body before meditation, remembering that you are preparing for communication with God. I find that washing my face and brushing my teeth before meditating also helps me wake up more fully, allowing me to be more alert during meditation.

Some of the same readings also suggest that you purify your mind before meditation, that you empty yourself of distractions and stressful tensions. Meditation may be less helpful if your mind is full of your other priorities and problems when you sit down to meditate. To this end, meditating shortly after waking up requires less mind-emptying than meditating after a day of activities and encounters. One way to help clear the mind is to read something uplifting or spiritually oriented before meditating. Some meditators read favorite passages in the Bible; others use inspirational poetry or spiritual writings. Listening to quiet music before meditating helps many people empty their minds of thoughts and become more receptive to nonverbal experiences. This is a matter of individual preference and experimentation. What works for you is best for you.

In the Western tradition sitting is the normal position for meditation, although some individuals find it conducive to meditation if they lie prone on a bed or on the floor. But because lying down often signals that the body is preparing for sleep, you may have difficulty training yourself to stay not only awake but alert during meditation in a prone position. Some like to meditate sitting cross-legged or lotus style on the floor, as in the Eastern tradition. Most older adults, however, find that the best meditation position is sitting in a comfortable, straight-backed chair in a relaxed but alert upright position. Hands may rest lightly in the lap, touching one another, or palms may rest on the upper legs. You will want to experiment to find a comfortable position that allows you to relax and yet be attentive.

You may want to use a specific routine for relaxing your entire body, especially early in your meditation experience. There are some audiotapes on the market to help with body relaxation. A progressive relaxation technique you may find helpful directs your attention to one part of your body at a time, usually beginning with the feet. It suggests you concentrate on relaxing that body part before progressing to the neighboring part. Using such a relaxation discipline has a desirable side benefit: it requires a level of concentration on the body that helps to dispel distracting thoughts and sounds.

In many readings unrelated to meditation, the Cayce readings recommend a simple head and neck exercise to improve the circulation in and around the neck and shoulders. So many people have found it helpful as a preparation to meditation that it has become associated with the Cayce approach to meditation. It is an excellent exercise at any time to relieve tension and aching in neck and shoulders. Briefly, the exercise has six head movements, each of which is performed three times:

> Sitting erect bend the head forward three times at least, then back as far as it may be bent three times; to the right side three times; then to the left side three times. Then circle the head and neck to the right three times, then to the left three times. Be consistent with this though, not just doing it occasionally. (no. 5404–1)

One of Cayce's readings for a sixty-five-year-old woman succinctly summarized this entire preparatory stage:

> Whatever manner of cleansing, physical, mental, or spiritual that seems necessary; that *do*; consistently. . . . Prepare thy mind and body as if ye would meet thy Lord and Master. Then sit in readiness, at designated periods. (no. 1152–9)

Stage Two: Attunement

The point of the second stage of meditation is to become attuned to God, to the infinite Creative Forces represented by God. While you are striving for that attunement, try to separate yourself from the desire to experience some particular personal benefit through meditation. Every action in this stage should be aimed at aligning yourself with the Infinite, which is prerequisite to any subsequent communication.

Begin the attunement stage with an opening prayer that is either silent or spoken aloud. Especially appropriate here are prayer statements of praise, thanksgiving, trust and faith, and protection. (Personal requests, prayers on forgiveness, and requests for others are offered during the third stage, after attunement is complete). An alternative to using your own opening prayer is using The Lord's Prayer.

After your opening prayer, clear your mind of distractions and direct your attention inward through your focus on an affirmation—

not on just the words, but on the feeling behind those words. The Cayce readings frequently say that little spiritual progress can be made without acting in accord with your ideal, so focusing on the ideal in an affirmation is especially helpful to attunement. You may use any of a variety of affirmations according to the specific concerns in your life at the time.

Another way to express the idea of focusing on an affirmation is feeling the essence of the affirmation, surrendering all your thoughts and other feelings to it. If it is consistent with your ideal, it is a key to the connection with God and his energy. Let it help you empty yourself of any distracting thoughts or tensions.

Once you sense you are single-minded in your focus and have given yourself over to the feeling of the affirmation, release the affirmation—not the qualities the affirmation has helped generate, but the words of the affirmation. Hold onto those qualities and the uplifting feelings created by the now-assimilated affirmation.

To keep your mind empty and undistracted, you may find it helpful to be aware of your breathing. Do not try to control your breathing rhythm in any way. It may become slower and reach deeper into your abdomen as you continue in silence, but you need not make any effort to alter it. Just attend to it as a focal point for your awareness.

After releasing the affirmation, begin a period of inner silence. The length of your total meditation period is determined largely by the length of this silence. You will be able to lengthen this period as you learn to keep your mind free of distracting thoughts and your body free of distracting sensations. The desirable state of consciousness throughout this silence is one of receptivity and alertness while you continue to be suffused with the qualities represented by the affirmation.

Your attentiveness is critical to your act of listening to God, aligning your consciousness with God. That doesn't mean that you will hear a voice speaking to you, but guidance and energy are available after alignment takes place at the end of the meditative process. During this alignment no reactions or sensations should be expected, although you may experience something. For example, you may feel a flow of energy pulsating through your body, moving from the bottom of your torso through the top of your head. But don't set up any expectations about specific sensations or experiences.

If mental or physical distractions occur, return to the affirmation or to observing the breathing. It may also be necessary to shift your physical position, especially if you are new to meditation. One of the implicit goals for your meditation period, however, should be to remain immobile as long as possible during the silence.

How long you remain in the quiet will be regulated by your own experience. At some point you will feel yourself beginning to emerge from the silence of your consciousness. The return of mental activity is sometimes accompanied by emotional feelings of love, of fulfillment, of thankfulness. Foster those feelings and let them fill your mind and body. Do not hurry into the next stage, but relish the contentment of this moment. For many people this feeling of being centered, relaxed, and in control of themselves is the primary objective of meditation.

Stage Three: Application

Application is the title given to this third stage because it implies that meditation does not end with the emergence from silence. You are reminded to apply the attunement you have achieved in order to communicate with God.

Remembering that you are listening to God in meditation, you may look for guidance and other useful information at this point, as you complete the attunement stage. While you are still in the relaxed state, enjoying the feelings of attunement, you may become aware of information related to some personal concern, even if you did not express your concern in your opening prayer.

You may offer prayers with personal requests and prayers on forgiveness at this time. The information you seek may come in words, in visual images, or in feelings. The information may not come now, but at a later time—later in the day, even after several days. You may not perceive any response at all. That may be either because you are not receiving any message or because you do not recognize the message. By working with meditation over a period of weeks and months, you begin to understand the information and signs you receive and start to distinguish between what is guidance and what is wishful thinking. In any case, you can continue in your practice of meditation knowing you will get the information or assistance you need if you persist.

The final activity of meditation is, according to Cayce, one of the most important—be a channel for helping someone else. At its simplest this takes the form of a prayer request for others, as described in the section on prayer. It is not your responsibility to tell God what to do to help another person, but rather to identify the person by name and ask that he or she be blessed or surrounded by God's love and light, for example, or to pray that God will do "what you know best to do." This kind of request for others may be extended to as many individuals as you want to include. The prayer might then conclude with a statement of thanksgiving and praise. Also, I find it helpful to restate my affirmation, as a reminder of my current focus.

Only after such prayers is the meditation period ended. If you're not used to sitting without movement for that long, or if you have any physical symptoms that may be aggravated by nonmovement, you may want to engage in some slow stretches and movement of your legs and body before you get up from your chair. This period of getting ready to move again also gives you the opportunity to make notes about the experience or about any information you received at the end of meditation.

The energy that can be tapped through meditation may, according to Cayce, be used for the physical healing of yourself and others. As with other methods of healing, precautions must be taken and certain restrictions observed. The reader interested in the use of meditation in healing, beyond the prayer suggestions just described, is referred to the book *Healing Through Meditation & Prayer*, by Meredith Ann Puryear.

I have presented enough information about meditation that you should be able to experience it for yourself. If you would like more detail on the process as well as on the philosophy of meditation according to the Cayce readings and other parallel sources, you will find it in the Mark Thurston book mentioned earlier, *The Inner Power of Silence: A Universal Way of Meditation.*

GETTING PERSONAL

Now it's time to integrate the affirmation, prayer, and meditation ideas through application and practice.

If you are already a practiced meditator, you can use this exercise to review your meditation and prayer activity. Would you like to experiment with the suggestions just presented?

If meditation is new to you, then use the following approach to meditation. Then consider incorporating it into your daily life. Be warned that if you try it, you'll like it!

Pick a time and place for a period of meditation, keeping in mind the suggestions previously outlined. Try for a setting where you will have the least distractions and an unhurried period of up to fifteen minutes. Select a chair that will allow you to sit comfortably erect with muscles relaxed throughout the body.

Review the affirmation for your ideal and the prayer you created in the earlier exercises in this chapter. Seeing now how you will incorporate them into your meditation period, you may wish to modify them or to select only parts of them for use. Have them available to read, if necessary, during the meditation period. Or use The Lord's Prayer instead.

Just prior to the appointed time, take whatever steps you feel are necessary for purifying the body. Avoid eating or drinking just before meditation, and consider washing your hands and face.

At the time of meditation, if you need a reminder of the process, review the following steps:

Preparation

1. Allow time to wind down with music or reading to help purify your mind and empty yourself of mental distractions.
2. Sit comfortably in the selected chair and relax your whole body, from the feet to the head, keeping the spine erect.

3. Use the head and neck exercise to release tension and increase circulation in the neck and the shoulders.

Attunement

4. When you feel relaxed, use your opening prayer to start the communication with God.
5. Focus on the affirmation for your ideal, repeating it and seeking the feeling behind it.
6. When you have that feeling, release the words of the affirmation and become aware of your breathing.
7. Allow yourself to drift into inner silence, but remain alert and receptive, holding the feeling of the affirmation.
8. Remain quiet for several minutes in this inner calm. Refocus on your affirmation or breathing if you find yourself getting distracted.

Application

9. As you emerge from the silence, notice any inner guidance or information that may come to you. Review it in your mind so you will recall it later.
10. Offer prayers on personal requests and on forgiveness. Listen for guidance.
11. Pray for others, give praise and thanks, and repeat your affirmation.
12. Emerge from meditation and make notes on anything you want to remember about the experience or information you received at the end of meditation.

Plan to repeat this experience daily, at about the same time, gradually increasing the length of time in inner silence. As you repeat the process, you may wish to modify it in some details to suit your own experience and needs, keeping to the general principles presented.

KEYS TO MEDITATION AND PRAYER

Books and courses have been prepared to help people understand and practice meditation. But remember that you must make your meditation process your own: "No one may tell another how to fall in love" (no. 2441–2). Here are a few key points to help you adapt meditation and prayer to your personality and your individuality and to help you accept your personal meditation experiences, whatever they are:

Meditation and prayer should become a habit. Probably more than any other spiritual practice, they contribute to your increasing understanding and enlightenment about yourself as a spiritual being; they are major contributors to the wisdom you gain as you age.

To make meditation a habit, emphasize regularity more than length or form. Try to associate it with an established time in your daily schedule, so that a habit can develop. And don't delay it until you are low in energy.

On the other hand, don't let habit become meaningless routine. Prayers and affirmations should remain up to date and meaningful. Alter them periodically to keep them fresh.

Remember that the purpose of the inner silence period is attunement, alignment with the Universal Forces. That is not the time for asking questions or seeking answers. Questions may follow the silence, and responses and guidance may come then or appear at a later time as an outcome of the meditation.

Don't anticipate any particular sensations or phenomena to occur during meditation. They may take place, but your meditation is not lacking if you never experience anything but silence.

If you don't seem to be communicating with God—that is, you don't seem to be getting any response to your requests or getting the assistance you seek—realize there can be many reasons for this, including the following:

Attunement will usually precede response—your meditation is intended to align you with the Universal Source of information that is God, and then you may get answers. You may need time and practice with the attunement process before you tap that Source.

Your request for help or information may need to be restated or even rethought. Have you been too general? Or even too specific? In what terms are you expecting the answer to be given? Try different expressions of your request from one meditation to another.

You do not recognize the information or answer. One way of simplifying the form of response is to state your request in a form requiring only a yes or no response. It is easier to interpret signs or symbols as favorable or unfavorable than to interpret information you have asked for in what, how, or why questions.

One final suggestion: You can extend your meditation experience by engaging in it more than once a day if you feel the need: when you are tense, nervous, or upset about something; when you have pain or discomfort; when you have need for reassurance and support. Suit your prayers and affirmations to the situation. That way you can realize the great sustaining power of meditation and prayer in every aspect of your life.

5

Dreams: Messages Not to Be Missed

All visions and dreams are given for the benefit of the individual, [if he would] but interpret them correctly. . . . Happy may he be [who] is able to say [he has] been spoken to through dream or vision.

EDGAR CAYCE reading no. 294–15

I AWOKE FROM A dream recently with the feeling that it was significant for me. This was my dream:

I am in the kitchen preparing a meal. I am taking a lot of time and care to cook chicken in a special way—cutting it up, adding seasonings, making a sauce. When that's done I prepare all kinds of other dishes. This is taking hours, and I am thoroughly enjoying myself. I realize that when we sit down to eat all this, we will finish it off in minutes, in spite of the hours of work. But that's all right because getting the meal ready is so satisfying in itself.

As I studied this dream off and on for several days, I found messages for me on four levels. Because I prepare many of the meals for our family of four, the dream has a literal message. Occasionally I spend an hour or two on a meal we consume in twenty minutes. The dream reminds me to enjoy the process of preparation.

Actually, that obvious message was not the first that came to mind as I studied the dream. Here I am, writing a book—a task extending over many months. Occasionally I think how wonderful it will be when the book is completed (the meal is ready). Yet whatever appreciation may be expressed for the completed book, it cannot compare with the inner rewards I am realizing as I write it. The dream helps me recognize those rewards along the way.

At sixty I am making the adjustment from outside employment to working at home, dividing time between family responsibilities and writing. As I take on more of the time-consuming processes involved in the care of our home and of two family members with disabilities, I am learning to find enjoyment and satisfaction in those activities, and this dream reinforces that.

The dream is helpful at still one more level, perhaps the most important level: in my dreams for several years, food has frequently represented spiritual nourishment—a source of energy and growth in my own progress toward Oneness with God. When I interpret the food preparation in this light, the dream takes on an even deeper message for me: relish the process of growing spiritually.

Who would have imagined that this simple dream could be relevant to so many areas of my life? I have appreciated every one of these messages many times since I had the dream.

One of the elders I talked with about the Edgar Cayce material had this to say about dream work:

> To me, the purpose of the dream is to help us understand what we have learned in time and space. And that learning depends on how well we have accepted what comes to us in dreams. They may show us our problem, what we have not handled properly, and give us an opportunity to correct ourselves.
>
> Working with dreams is simple if you look for the truth in the dream. That truth will be found in your life. That's what Edgar Cayce said: "Look for the truth." And we can do this all our lives, because dreams are with us from our first breath to our last.

The truth revealed to me in my dream is that I will find satisfaction and fulfillment in the processes in my life, not just in the outcomes. Another level of truth the dream has for me is that one pattern may take many forms in my life, and to change the pattern, I may need to attend to several areas. For much of my life, I was impatient with most processes, eager for completion and results.

Discussing this dream illustrates the value dream work can have in your later years. You even gain some advantage in dream work as you grow older: you have less need or desire to jump out of bed first thing, giving you a better chance at recalling dreams. You may have a more consistent sleep pattern at night, and you may nap occasionally during the day and evening, giving you plenty of opportunities for dreams and dreamlike images. Here are reports of three experiences of an eighty-five-year-old woman who says that they were not dreams, that she rarely dreams:

After sitting alone in her room one afternoon, she said she had been talking to someone and found out that her sister wasn't in a Denver nursing home anymore, but was in a hospital in Steubenville, Ohio. She asked about the possibility of going to visit her there.

A few days later—again after a long quiet time in her chair in her room—she said that her Uncle Carl had come to see her and said he was ready to take her away with him. He said if she wasn't ready to leave right then, he would come back later for her.

Several months later, after a morning alone in her room where she had no radio, television, or telephone, she said she was glad to hear news that morning about her hometown of Weirton, West Virginia. They were selling things, such as properties. She couldn't remember any more.

Before you can help a dreamer with interpretation, you need some knowledge of the dreamer and what is happening in his or her life. The following facts will be helpful in seeing meaning in the preceding experiences, which I will refer to as dreams:

The dreams were experienced during the daytime, when the woman frequently spends time dozing or drifting in and out of sleep, either on her bed or in her chair. Such periods between wakefulness and sleep are often characterized by a hypnagogic state, during which the conscious and subconscious minds are exchanging places in dominance. Dreamlike images often occur. This woman says she wasn't dreaming; according to her, she seldom dreams.

This woman has very limited interests, reduced physical and mental abilities, and few means by which to entertain herself. Sometimes she expresses boredom and seems to be waiting for something to happen.

The sister lived most of her childhood and married life in Weirton, across the Ohio River from Steubenville, and the dreamer herself lived in Weirton until she was married. For many of those early years, the only hospital in the area was in Steubenville.

The sister, also in her eighties, has disabilities in memory, speech, and thinking very similar to those of the dreamer. Since their declines in memory, they have fallen out of touch.

Carl, her father's brother, with whom she was not especially close, was the most recent of her relatives to die, and that was of leukemia at the age of ninety-four, about five years before the dream. When asked if Carl seemed old, she said he was young—probably the same age as the person questioning her (who was in her late fifties). Did she think he was dead? "Oh no! He was right here in this room!" she said, pointing toward the top of a door.

Considering this background, one interpretation of the three dreams taken as a whole is that the woman is preparing herself for her transition at death. The sister may represent one aspect of herself, giving herself up to complete care. The uncle may be a less well known part of herself, helping her see that everything is well on the other side and encouraging her not to hang onto life. He may be, at least symbolically, a messenger from the other side, ready to help her make her transition, but also reminding her that she is in control of when she does it. The sale of properties in her hometown suggests that material goods could be disposed of if she were "home."

Part of this interpretation of the second dream was shared with her, and she seemed to accept the hopefulness of it. She still insisted, however, that she hadn't been dreaming.

Thus dream work can be helpful not only in the ongoing activity of your life, but also in helping you accept the transition beyond. You can also help other elders understand their dreams.

Thoughtful dream work can be an excellent demonstration of the growing wisdom of your later years. In fact, to ignore dreams when you are attempting to grow spiritually through other means is like "running down the spiritual path with one eye closed," according to theologian Harmon Bro in his book *Dreams in the Life of Prayer and Meditation.*

OPENING ANOTHER COMMUNICATION LINE TO GOD

Two concepts from the Edgar Cayce readings underscore the value of dreams as a channel for messages from God. First, the reading quoted at the beginning of the chapter says that all dreams are for the benefit of the individual. That is, they contain information about the dreamer's life and health that will be helpful to the dreamer once it is interpreted and applied, and, by extension, they contain nothing that will be detrimental. Even dream events and symbols that may not seem constructive turn out to be helpful and hopeful (key Cayce criteria) when interpreted in the context of the dreamer's life.

Elders are often the target for information, suggestions, and advice from many sources—family members, other elders, clergy, physicians, newspaper articles, TV shows, and, of course, books like this one. Such information is often based on a stereotype of what "elderly" is, or, at the other extreme, based on the experience of a specific elderly individual whose situation may be nothing like yours. How do you sort out all these ideas and consider them in light of who you are and what your specific needs and interests may be? Not only can God help you to sort through such information, but God can provide guidance about things in your life of which you aren't even consciously aware. A dream is one of the most versatile media God has to get through to you with messages you may not get any other way. In the words of one of my elder conversation partners—who also happens to be a theologian—"I sometimes get significant dreams and take them seriously, because I'm convinced it's one way that God uses to communicate with us."

The second concept from the readings that supports the value of dream work is that nothing important ever happens to you without first being previewed in your dreams. This helps to explain why you might find yourself saying, "I knew that was going to happen!" or "I'm not really surprised," even when the occurrence was otherwise unexpected. Your subconscious mind had been prepared by prior dreams. By conscientious work with your dreams, you can bring more of this subconscious knowledge to the conscious level and be even better prepared. As you face a future where your physical, mental, and spiritual challenges may increase, you can prepare for them only if you can anticipate them without trying to plan for every possible contingency. God's dream messages can keep you focused on those issues that need your attention.

In brief, because dreams provide a significant way to receive information from the creative forces of God, dream work is suggested as one of the spiritual components—along with ideals and purposes, prayer and meditation—for building the foundation of your later years. Dreams are indeed messages not to be missed.

True, the messages often come veiled and may appear unfathomable, and a dream can usually be interpreted in more than one way. Why does God do this? Why not give you the straight story during waking hours? Possible reasons include the following:

> Your most important human gift is your free will. You choose which information you want to pay attention to. Dream information is always available, but first you have to choose to remember it and then choose to interpret it.
>
> If you were to get the straight story during waking hours, how would you separate it from the products of your conscious thoughts and imagination? Dreams at least do not have to compete with the conscious mind for attention, although they are filtered through your own unconscious mind, still requiring your discernment.
>
> Dreams often contain symbols and metaphors, so you can inter-

pret dreams at different levels and see patterns in your life, not just reflections of specific waking circumstances.

Dreams may give you messages you don't want to hear—you are overweight, smoking too much, need to repair a relationship. When you are serious about your dream work, it's more difficult to ignore such messages than if they occur to you while you are awake—as they probably do, perhaps to little effect.

Whatever the reasons for dreams having their unique qualities and forms of information, they are ready to yield their messages to those who will make the effort to record and interpret them on a regular basis.

GETTING THE MESSAGE

Some people say, "But I don't dream" or "I know I dream but I never remember my dreams." And so they ask to be excused from dream work. The fact is that everyone dreams. Only some remember their dreams, and fewer still look for meaning in their remembered dreams. Actually, the frequency of dream recall and the amount of detail recalled can be greatly increased when the dreamer is motivated to recall, records his or her dreams, and follows through with interpretation and application.

Several years ago I was a member of a dream group that met monthly to share dreams and help one another with interpretation. A man who accompanied his wife frequently declared, "I don't dream." No one asked him to change his attitude or to try to recall dreams, and he continued in that passive attitude for months. But obviously he came to accept the fact that he was probably dreaming like everyone else, and could remember his dreams if he wanted to, because finally he came to a session and told us about a dream—it had recurred several times—and he asked the group's help in interpretation. The dream was unusual and had great significance for him. From then on he was an active participant in the group.

In my experience the universe is very responsive to my intentions about dreams, and many others feel the same way. When I would like to begin remembering my dreams, the response may not be instantaneous—that is, I may not recall a dream the first night I seek to. Facetiously, I say the universe doesn't believe I'm really serious yet, so it is waiting for me to get serious and ask again, and maybe again. But if I am persistent in seeking my dreams, within a few days I will begin to recall them.

When I get to a period when I'm remembering my dreams but not recording, interpreting, or applying them, the recall begins to fade, until I realize I am not remembering them with any regularity.

If you are seriously interested in working with your dreams, here are several preparations that will let God know you're serious:

1. *Prepare your dream-recording materials.* First, decide how you will record your dreams. The most direct approach is to have paper and pen or pencil within easy reach beside your bed. Demonstrate your intent to record a dream by writing the date and any questions you are posing for a dream response. Because you will want to keep an ongoing record of your dreams, I suggest you use a notebook or journal for them. In the exercises that follow, you can use the notebook you have started for this book and change to a dream notebook later.

   If you have difficulty writing when you first awaken, consider getting a tape recorder with a small plug-in microphone that has an on/off switch. Set the recorder to record before you go to sleep, record the date and questions, if any, and then turn the microphone switch off. When you want to record, simply grab the microphone, flip the switch, and begin.

2. *When you awaken, refrain from moving for several seconds.* Give yourself time to recall a dream, and, if you do, to review the main details of it in your mind. Once you begin to move, you are less likely to remember your dreams. If you go over it once, you are more likely to be able to record it in your journal or on tape.

3. *Record your dream.* Write down or dictate as many details as you can remember about your dream. Include any feelings

you had when you woke up and any first impressions you have about the meaning of the dream or any of its symbols or events. If you recall more than one dream, number them in the sequence in which they occurred, even if you do not recall and record them in that order.

4. *Later, review and expand if possible.* After you have been awake for a while, you may recall other details of the dream, especially if you review what you have already recorded. You may also add information about events or emotions experienced the day before the dream that seem to be relevant. For example, if your dream took place in or near water, you may want to record that you had gone swimming earlier that day.

One advantage of growing older is that you have more opportunities to receive dreams and dream images, such as those reported for the eighty-five-year-old woman earlier in this chapter. As part of your routine, you may schedule a nap on your bed during the day, or you may simply fall asleep in your chair while reading or watching TV. Because there are possibilities for dreams at these times, or for other images in the hypnagogic states you pass through as you drift between dozing and consciousness, plan to record these dreams or dream images, noting the time and where you were when they occurred. View all these rest and sleep opportunities as your added special times for dream messages.

GETTING PERSONAL

Because you know that immediate application is the best way to make the activity your own, take time now to prepare for recording dreams beginning tonight. Decide how you will do your recording and where you will put your notebook or tape recorder. As a reminder to yourself at bedtime, lay a note on your pillow now to prepare yourself for recording your dreams.

When you are ready for bed and sleep, record the date in your notebook or on the tape, and place everything where you can easily reach it when you awaken. Take a few minutes to review the events and feelings of your day.

As you fall asleep, instruct yourself (and the universe) that you are planning to remember and record at least one dream when you wake up. Be convinced that you will do this, and that the dream will have a helpful message for you. You may state this assurance as an affirmation, such as, "When I awake, I will remember and record a dream with a helpful message for me."

Make the suggested mechanical preparations for tonight's dreams now, and then follow through tomorrow by recording tonight's dream. Make the same preparations on the next several nights, recording whatever you can the following mornings.

You may remember a dream from tonight's sleep, or it may take several nights before you have one to record. Be persistent in your preparation and affirmation, and you will soon have many dreams with which to work.

DECIPHERING THE MESSAGE

Once your efforts in preparing for and recording your dreams are rewarded, you can begin the most fascinating part of dream work—interpretation. Single dreams may be interpreted immediately, especially if the dream or the dream request has some urgency; delayed interpretation allows more time to analyze and process, look at earlier dreams, and perhaps get the assistance of others who work with dreams.

The interpretation process looks not only at obvious dream content, such as people, settings, words, and events, but also at themes, symbols, feelings, and patterns, either in single dreams or in a collection of dreams from the same person. This section first presents several principles about dreams discussed in the Cayce readings. Following these principles is an outline of steps for interpreting your dreams.

Dreams can be interpreted correctly in several different ways. One frequent misconception is that there is a single correct interpretation for every dream. As illustrated in my own dream reported at the beginning of this chapter, you may interpret your dreams on several different levels—often on a physical, a mental, and a spiritual level; sometimes for several different areas of your life; sometimes for the future as well as for the present.

The quality and value of your dreams depends on your intent. The more spiritually attuned you are—if you, for example, work with spiritual ideals, life's purposes, meditation, and prayer—the more likely it is that your dream content will be drawn from helpful universal sources. If your life is shaped primarily by physical circumstances and mental activity, you may expect to find your dream content drawn largely from your own subconscious. And if you are looking for information for personal gain without personal growth, for purposes related only to you and not others, your dreams may become barren, and recall may cease.

You are the best interpreter of your own dreams, if you will learn the principles and steps of interpretation, and also allow intuition to operate. If you are not thus prepared, then others with experience may help you interpret your dreams, hedging suggestions with, "If it were *my* dream . . ." and frequently asking you for information or feelings that will make the interpretation ring true.

You cannot interpret another's dreams unless you have considerable knowledge of the dreamer. As evident from the dreams discussed earlier, dream content is highly related to the dreamer's intent, as well as to what is going on in his or her life. The images and symbols may come from the dreamer's unique experience rather than from a repertoire of symbols frequently encountered in dreams. For example, in the Cayce readings interpreting dreams, the act of swimming may be interpreted as making spiritual progress. To interpret a dream of mine that involves swimming, however, you have to know that I swim several times a week for exercise. Therefore in my dreams swimming may represent a much more mundane aspect of my life. The dreams of the woman discussed early in this chapter could not have been interpreted at all without knowledge of her circumstances and background. Even then the interpretation is limited because the dreamer was not able to participate much in the interpretation, and not at all in identifying the dream's purpose, which plays an important part in its interpretation.

Dreams are of three broad categories, corresponding to their origin in the physical, the mental, or the spiritual. Dreams produced from physical causes reflect conditions in the body, frequently the digestive system. Dreams with mental causes are frequently problem-solving dreams, helping you become more effective in managing the day-to-day issues of life. Spiritual dreams attempt to help you understand the purpose of life and accept a stronger relationship with God. Some dreams include content in more than one of these areas.

Dreams contain three types of symbols: literal, representational, and visionary. Literal symbols directly reflect the objects, people, and events you experience in waking life. (Images of your house, for example, represent your house.) Representational symbols are those where an object or event represents another object or event, as a metaphor does. (A national flag might represent the country or the idea of patriotism; a cross might represent Jesus or the Christian church; and feet might represent support or, in a play on words, understanding.) Some visionary symbols (Cayce's term) appear to be drawn from a universal source (such as the archetypes referred to by Carl Jung), and others are created spontaneously during the dream. Visionary symbols are images or situations with meanings that cannot be expressed by literal or representational symbols, concepts and feelings far beyond their apparent form. (The complex symbol of food preparation in my dream had a visionary quality to it, in addition to its literal and representational qualities, because it awakened in me some ideas and emotions about processes and products far beyond the everyday cooking of a meal.)

The information and guidance emerging from dream interpretation is verified through application. Dream work is not intended as an intellectual exercise, like decoding cryptograms. Dreams are intended to be instructive and helpful in meeting your daily challenges. In fact, the best way to find out if a dream has been interpreted correctly is to try out your interpretation. For example, in my dream of food preparation, if my interpretation is correct, I should allow myself to enjoy the processes as well as the products. This may require some initial reminders about the dream until I assimilate that idea and awaken the feelings that go with it. When I spontaneously experience the joy of the processes, as I increasingly do, I have proven the validity of my interpretation. Also, a dream may be clarified or its interpretation verified through later dreams or through responses to requests in meditation asking about the dream.

Dreams respond to the suggestions and concerns you express before sleeping. Earlier I described the preparations for recalling and recording dreams, pointing out that the intent to recall and record a dream has a direct impact on whether or not you do recall. You can take this idea a step further by asking that your dreams address a certain issue. For several weeks before my food preparation dream, I asked for guidance on making a smooth adjustment to new responsibilities and circumstances in my life. That dream seems to be at least part of the answer. After a recent physical injury, I expressed the need to understand the lessons of that injury; I have received helpful responses from dreams as well as waking experiences. Remember that a key to the responsiveness of dreams is attunement through the ideals and through meditation and prayer. Harmon Bro's book *Dreams in the Life of Prayer and Meditation* is especially helpful in understanding and working with the relationship among these spiritual building blocks.

To put these principles and ideas into action, you may find the following steps helpful in the interpretation of a dream:

1. Read through or listen to your record of the dream, together with any other information you have recorded about preceding conditions, feelings, and questions. Add to your record any new impressions or feelings you have about the dream or its meaning.

2. Select what you see as highly important—a word, object, person, color, event, symbol; more than one element might be highly important. In my dream reported at the beginning of the chapter, food preparation was obviously important, as well as time.

3. Capture the essence of the dream in one or more of these ways:

    Give the dream a title. (For my dream, *Preparation Time*.)

    Restate the dream in its simplest form. ("I am enjoying preparing the meal in spite of the long preparation time and the short consumption time.")

    Define the theme of the dream ("Enjoy the process as well as the product.")

    These should help you concentrate on the heart of the dream, although other symbols and details should be considered in the final interpretation.

4. Consider the dream from different levels:

    Look for literal meaning. (For my dream, the enjoyment of meal preparation itself.)

    Look for spiritual meanings: in physical life, mental life, spiritual life. (Several symbolic interpretations of my dream were described.)

5. Relate dream work to other insights or expressions:

    While you are working on the dream, other thoughts and images may come to mind. Write them down and consider them in your interpretation.

    If you spontaneously remember the dream later, notice what is going on at the time you think about the dream. That may give you some insight into interpreting the dream.

6. Consider the primary symbols in the dream and the meanings they carry for you. As you continue to work with your dreams, you will begin to recognize recurring symbols. You will develop your own vocabulary of symbols personal to you, and gradually supplement them with the more traditional and archetypal symbols that appear.

7. Record your interpretation and your plan for application and action when appropriate. You can verify your interpretation by starting to use the information in your life. You can also

look to meditation and new dreams for verification or clarification by requesting help during meditation or before sleep.

More detailed information on dream interpretation and guidance is in Mark Thurston's *Dreams: Tonight's Answers for Tomorrow's Questions.*

GETTING PERSONAL

If you have recorded any dreams, use the preceding principles and steps to interpret at least one dream. Make notes in your notebook of the activities you find most useful in the interpretation process.

If you have not recorded any dreams, write down a scene from a movie or TV program, a scene from a book, or an incident that occurred in real life. Describe it as if it were a dream. Then proceed to follow the preceding principles and steps to interpret the scene or incident as if it were your dream.

Every night before you go to sleep, continue affirming your interest in your dreams and your intention of working with the information you receive. Be sure to allow yourself a good night's sleep!

DREAM MESSAGES IN THE LATER YEARS

The later years are accompanied by some concerns and problems that come with aging. Guidance on these issues can be obtained through persistent work with dreams. For example, your body may operate less efficiently or your senses may require more assistance to do their job. You can use dreams as a means for discovering physical problems before they become severe and for getting help in prevention and care. In the readings on dreams given to twelve people age fifty or older, Cayce finds several instances of disturbing dreams resulting from digestive upsets—"poor assimilations," in his words. This is one of the most frequent physical complaints of older people, so it is not surprising that this condition affects some of their dreams.

Elders often have major decisions to make: What should I do with my time after retirement—find other paid work, volunteer, take it easy? Where shall I live now that my spouse is dead and my family has moved away? How should I take care of my financial resources—invest them safely myself, use a financial adviser, spend more of them on myself? Add dream work to whatever approach you use to deliberate such issues, keeping your life ideals and purpose in mind.

The challenge of dealing with our interpersonal relationships never ends, although it may take different forms as you grow older. For example, when your predominant relationship has for many years been with one individual, how do you compensate for the loss of that relationship when that person is gone? How do you adjust to changes in your role with your children as they also grow older, particularly if they try to become your advice-giving "parents"? Dreams can help with such questions.

As you physically age, your spiritual development might assume a higher priority. Dream work is an invaluable building block for your spiritual development and thus for your soul growth. And as an extension of that growth, you can gain increasing understanding and acceptance of the physical death that not only claims more and more of your friends and contemporaries, but also lies in your own future. According to Cayce, dreams give you the opportunity to sample death before you experience it. He says that sleep is a "shadow of . . . that state called death" (no. 5754–1) and reminds us that death itself is merely a transition from one dimension of living to another dimension of living. If sleeping and dreaming allow me to rehearse death, I choose to enhance my understanding and acceptance of it by actively working with my dreams. That way I won't miss many messages!

6

Attitudes and Emotions: The Choice Is Yours

For mind is the builder and that which we think upon may become crimes or miracles. For thoughts are things and as their currents run through [our] experience these become barriers or stepping-stones, dependent on the manner in which these are laid.

EDGAR CAYCE reading no. 906–3

As AN OBSERVER OF human nature, have you noticed that most casual conversation reflects feelings more than facts? For example, I recently made note of these fragments of conversations in a restaurant:

Two young women:

"I really shouldn't get any dessert. I'm beginning to look like a slob."

"You're crazy! You look just like the rest of us—granted that may not be too great!"

Two elder women, probably in their sixties:

"It's so good to see you again after all this time! I'm glad I bumped into you in the store."

"I don't seem to get out much anymore. I don't like to ask anyone for a ride. It's such a bother."

"I'd be delighted to run by and pick you up. Maybe we could catch a movie sometime."

Two fortyish men in business suits:

"This sure isn't my day. I could've knocked a few heads this morning! Nothing got done!"

"They'll catch up this afternoon. They know about the tight schedule."

"They don't care if we blow the deal!"

"They want it as much as you do, Jack."

You hear a surprising range of feelings in the brief exchanges between these people—self-criticism, loneliness, sympathy, helpfulness, anger, optimism—attitudes about themselves, about others, about circumstances they deem important.

These words expressed in conversation are more than just a chance to share or complain or let off steam. Some of them represent views that are well settled in the speakers' minds—attitudes and emotions of more than momentary consequence. Put that factor into the middle of this law: "The spirit is life, the mind is the builder, the physical is the result." Go a step further and consider the quotation that begins this chapter: what we think about may become "crimes or miracles," and "thoughts are things and . . . become barriers or stepping-stones." Attitudes and emotions wield enormous power in our lives, guarding as they do that mental bridge between the infinite potential of the spiritual and the limited experience of the physical.

You have chosen the attitudes you hold, believe in, and express, and you can choose to change them. They are not visited upon you by a mysterious outside force, although you may not be aware of when and how you acquired them. As you look at yourself from the favorable position of later years, you can identify your attitudes more clearly, and can probably recognize some of the effects they have had in your life. That means you can also take the opportunity to make them more consistent with "miracles" and "stepping-stones" than with "crimes" or "barriers."

The Cayce readings address attitudes and emotions probably

more frequently than any other subject except physical health. This chapter presents a variety of issues to illustrate the range of the Cayce approach to the subject. First, you will examine some of your attitudes about yourself, using as a focus your attitudes about the prospects of aging. Then I will review basic concepts and principles from the Cayce readings about attitudes and emotions, and how they affect you physically and whether they change as you get older. Following those fundamentals, I will explore the peculiar dynamics of attitudes toward others, and follow that with a discussion of forgiveness. I will then look at the paradoxical emotion of fear, including the fear of death. Finally, I will summarize some ideas for controlling and managing attitudes and emotions.

YOUR ATTITUDES ABOUT AGING AND YOURSELF

In her book *Our Best Years*, actress Helen Hayes says:

> What becomes fragile when we age is not our bodies so much as our *egos*. We don't *like* ourselves in the altered state. . . . Self-denial is self-deceit. If we employ that kind of negative mentality, how can we expect to be received with open arms by the world out there? Wanting to lose track of time, as so many depressed elderly do, is a sure road to deterioration. Why look at old age as a personal insult?

In Chapter 1 you examined your views of what it is like to grow older, trying to separate the facts from the myths about aging. Take a closer look now at your attitudes about yourself as you grow older.

GETTING PERSONAL

Table 4 will help you inventory your attitudes about your own aging. As with earlier self-inventories, consider how strongly you agree or disagree with each statement, and then circle the answer in the column that best represents your view of the statement, ignoring for now the value of the number you are circling. The right score is the one that truly represents your feelings today.

Table 4
Self-Inventory: As I Grow Older...

For each statement, circle the answer in the column that best represents your current level of agreement or disagreement.

Strongly disagree
Disagree
Undecided
Agree
Strongly agree

		Strongly agree	Agree	Undecided	Disagree	Strongly disagree
1.	I will be able to take care of my day-to-day affairs for a long time to come.	5	4	3	2	1
2.	I see the dangers and hazards to older people steadily increasing around me.	1	2	3	4	5
3.	I feel very much alive, with plenty going on in my life to keep me active and interested.	5	4	3	2	1
4.	I spend a lot of time worrying about what will happen to me as I grow older.	1	2	3	4	5
5.	I would like to have more opportunities to help other people in tangible ways.	5	4	3	2	1
6.	I feel I can enjoy life more and find more satisfaction in life now than ever before.	5	4	3	2	1
7.	I often feel like my time in this life is running out.	1	2	3	4	5
8.	I find myself resenting people my age who are more active and interesting than I am.	1	2	3	4	5
9.	I still want to learn brand-new skills or learn about subjects I have never studied.	5	4	3	2	1
10.	I don't anticipate any serious decline in my physical health from now on.	5	4	3	2	1
11.	At my age there's no point to seeking and initiating new friendships.	1	2	3	4	5
12.	I am increasingly afraid of becoming disabled in some way and a burden to someone else.	1	2	3	4	5

After you complete the self-inventory, score it by adding up the numbers you have circled. Find the total in one of the following ranges:

48–60: You appear to have consistently positive attitudes about yourself as you experience aging. You tend to be optimistic about your life right now, interested in continuing to have new experiences and friends, and confident about yourself and your future. You tend to have a positive self-image and view your health and abilities with assurance. You seem to be managing your attitudes and emotions about aging very well.

36–47: You appear to have mixed attitudes about yourself as you experience aging, or you are neutral or undecided on many of these concerns. If you scored 1 or 2 on any items, look at those statements to see what issues they deal with. They may reflect specific attitudes and emotions you may want to evaluate more closely.

24–35: You appear to have unfavorable attitudes about yourself and your life as you grow older. You may be especially concerned about your health or your physical abilities, and the constraints they may impose on you now or later. You may feel easily irritated by other people or by occurrences that upset your normal life. You may feel that life is now passing you by, and you may not even care. Remember that the attitudes you choose represent the life you will live. Choosing and developing different attitudes can change your life. Look at the statements on which you scored 1 or 2, and consider them candidates for possible change.

12–23: You appear to be quite negative about yourself and your life as you grow older. You seem to have a lot of concerns—about health, safety, disruption of routine, other people, time running out, and so on. The attitudes you choose represent the life you will live, so choosing and developing different attitudes can change your life. Look at the statements on which you scored 1 or 2; you may want to consider them candidates for possible change.

———————————

Now that you have explored some of the elements that constitute one of your own attitudes, let's step back to take a broader view of the dynamics of attitudes and emotions as presented in the Cayce readings.

EXPLORING YOUR ATTITUDES AND EMOTIONS

An attitude is a point of view about a subject, a person, or a situation. An attitude will lead the person holding it to act or react in ways consistent with the attitude. For example, a restaurant customer's attitude of impatience will probably increase his internal stress as he waits; it may also lead to expressions of impatience to others, including the servers, other employees, and owners; and it may result in a smaller tip. Anger may result in errors, poor judgment, and even physical violence. Joy may cause a person to smile or sing or walk with more spring in her step, enhance her feeling of well-being and satisfaction, and even heal—spiritually, mentally, and physically.

You choose the attitudes you hold, sometimes by conscious choice, but more often by unconscious reaction to other influences. For example, I may consciously choose to cooperate with the other members of a committee to agree on a budget, even if a pet project of mine has to be scrapped to maintain solvency. On the other hand, if the committee seems to me to take a lot of unnecessary time to deal with its agenda, that may well mean I have an underlying attitude of impatience with its process—an attitude I have not consciously chosen. Recognizing that attitude, I could choose to replace it with one of loving patience—if I'm willing to discontinue the habit of impatience that may be lodged in my personality. And it is in my personality—my outward-appearing character in this life—that such an attitude is housed, not in my individuality—the evolving character of my soul.

Occasionally an attitude you are trying to hold is overridden by a conflicting attitude stemming from current circumstances, perhaps your physical condition. For instance, I may try hard at being patient with myself and with others, and be successful at it most of the time. But when I am dealing with back pain or a pounding headache or plain weariness, my patience is suddenly nowhere within reach, replaced by its opposite for the time being. One of my elder conversation partners who is normally very even tempered and gentle admitted, "On a day when I feel low, I try to stay pretty much to myself, so I'm not tempted to lash out because of my imbalance." This natural tendency to allow temporary physical or mental imbalances to divert you from your intended attitudes reinforces your need for staying in good physical and mental health.

The Cayce material differentiates between attitudes and emotions. Whereas attitudes are perspectives and tendencies to react in certain ways, emotions are deeper, more diffuse feelings, often triggering patterns of reacting that have developed over at least this lifetime. Emotions such as fear, anger, and anxiety may be triggered directly by some occurrence or more indirectly through a related attitude. For example, fear may be triggered by a perception of danger or physical attack, or by persistent attitudes of worry, loneliness, or self-condemnation.

Emotional reactions sometimes seem far more intense than the situation warrants. An emotion is an accumulation of feelings and reactions built up over years of experiences that shape them. When you tap into this deep pool, you may suddenly release a flood of emotion.

Furthermore, according to Cayce, some emotional patterns are carried over from previous lives, fed by experiences you cannot remember. For example, my excessive anxiety about not having enough time may reflect a previous existence cut short.

An important part of your work on the spiritual path is identifying your attitudes and emotions and understanding what triggers them and what sustains them.

THE PHYSICAL EFFECTS OF
ATTITUDES AND EMOTIONS

Spiritual attunement is blocked by some attitudes and emotions. An attitude of racial or sexual bias is incompatible with the law of Oneness; an emotion of unreasonable fear is incompatible with the continuous availability of God's resources. And good mental health is directly related to attitudes and emotions and how they are managed.

As to physical effects, the word *psychosomatic* is more than one hundred years old, but only recently have most people come to accept the fact that at least some illness is emotional in origin. Now growing in acceptance is the affirmative side of this body/mind relationship: *You can maintain wellness and overcome physical ailments through your positive attitudes and emotions.* Examples of healing through a therapy for the emotions and the mind are the experiences reported in *Getting Well Again* by oncologist Dr. O. Carl Simonton and psychotherapist Stephanie Matthews-Simonton, working with cancer patients, and the recovery from a crippling disease with a survival rate of one in five hundred, reported by editor Norman Cousins in *Anatomy of an Illness as Perceived by the Patient.* In his book *Who Gets Sick*, Blair Justice reports that authorities in the field of immunology now acknowledge that your resistance to infections, allergies, autoimmunities, and even cancer can be changed by your attitudes, by stress, and by depression.

According to the Cayce material, the emotions affect the physical body through seven endocrine glands, which lie in a line from the groin to the top of the brain. These seven glands are so critical to the spiritual attunement process that Cayce referred to their locations as the seven spiritual centers. They are as follows:

the gonads, in the groin area
the cells of Leydig, in the lower abdomen
the adrenal glands, at the solar plexus
the thymus gland, in the heart area
the thyroid gland, in the throat area
the pituitary gland, in the forehead
the pineal gland, at the top of the head

Each center is not only the locus of a ductless gland, secreting hormones into the bloodstream, but is also a point where nerves connect in a plexus. According to Cayce, these glands act as transducers, converting the energy coming into the gland to another form of energy, which then goes out.

Eastern tradition refers to these seven centers as chakras and to the energy that flows from the lowest to the highest of these as kundalini. As attunement takes place, the meditator sometimes becomes aware of this energy flow. The words of The Lord's Prayer, according to Cayce, help to move the energy through the seven centers, making the prayer especially helpful as a prelude to meditation.

Only recently has medical and physiological science begun to investigate and explain the complex functioning of this glandular system. In *Who Gets Sick*, Justice points out that the 1977 Nobel prize for physiology or medicine was awarded to Guillemin and Schally of the United States for their research in the role of hormones in the chemistry of the body. Working independently, they demonstrated that "a series of tiny molecules that are made in the brain's hypothalamus . . . travel to the body's 'master gland,' the pituitary, where they then affect the functioning of our thyroids, adrenals, gonads, and the very course of our somatic growth." This is consistent with Cayce's readings, which suggest that the endocrine glands not only perform their own unique functions, but that they interact with one another and instruct the rest of the body to react according to established patterns. Repetitions of those physiological signal patterns also create reaction patterns of behavior and emotions. Ultimately, a situation that mentally triggers the adrenals, for example, may initiate a complex reaction pattern that may include anger, a rise in blood pressure, an increase in breathing rate, dilation of the pupils in the eyes, and a wild array of mental images and other emotions drawn from past experience.

In summary, then, your physical being is the product not only of your body as you have nurtured it over your lifetime, but also of the attitudes and emotions you have nurtured. Following the logic of "the spirit is life; the mind is the builder; the physical is the result," those mental attitudes and emotions are in turn the outgrowth of what you have done about your spiritual purposes and ideals, and your physical condition has resulted from those mental patterns. Thus have you become what your mind has habitually drawn to it and dwelt upon. You have created your own present physical condition—an idea that may seem difficult to accept.

Two excerpts from readings dramatize this Cayce principle. The first is for a sixty-four-year-old man suffering from cancer of the mouth (where his attitudes find verbal expression). After recommending some dietary and spinal treatments, the reading adds:

> Keep the mental attitude constructive. Do not belittle. Do not condemn. Do not give vent to *any* activity that is not creative, constructive. Healing must come from within. The healing must be in the mind and the soul if the body will be clean. (no. 2764–1)

The second excerpt extends the effect of attitudes to a consideration of longevity:

> [As] the attitude, the purposes and ideals . . . are set and worked towards, we may increase the life existence, [the] life experience in the present. (no. 1179–11)

So if the down side is that today's physical condition comes from yesterday's attitudes and emotions, the up side is that you can shape tomorrow's physical condition with today's attitudes and emotions.

"NATURAL" CHANGES IN YOUR ATTITUDES?

Maybe if you just forget about your attitudes, they will mellow as you age. Or maybe the changes will go in the opposite direction, and you will get more ornery with age. What are the natural effects of aging on your attitudes and emotions?

In *Passages* Gail Sheehy points out that your attitudes about your way of living are shaped by four areas of perception, which may change as you pass from one period of life to another: (1) your inner sense of self in relation to others; (2) the balance of safety versus danger you feel in your life; (3) your feelings about how much time you have left; and (4) the balance between a sense of aliveness and a feeling of stagnation. The passage you make into your later years may have a considerable impact on these perceptions. In the self-inventory of Table 4, three-fourths of the statements address these four perceptions directly: items 2, 3, 5, 6, 7, 8, 9, 11, and 12. You may want to look at your responses on those statements to see where you are relative to these four sensitive perception areas. Ask yourself if your feelings in these areas have changed in recent years. If so, have they changed with your permission? Maybe you want an opportunity to reconsider them.

So simply getting older can influence your feelings, as you have probably experienced, but you can choose to control the effect of even these influences.

One popular myth about your attitudes as you age says you can expect to undergo a radical personality change as you reach your later years. Some purveyors of this myth suggest that your least desirable behaviors come to the fore and are amplified. According to this theory, if I have a tendency to be critical of others, but curb it reasonably well most of my life, I can expect I will become supercritical as I pass through my sixties and seventies. Other sources suggest that you can expect an even more radical change of personality, exhibiting nonconstructive attitudes quite unlike any previous behavior.

Not true, according to the most comprehensive recent research. Much of the best information now available about the effects of aging comes from the studies conducted by the Gerontology Research Center in Baltimore, Maryland. About thirty years ago this monumental program began to track the physical and mental health of many individuals over a long period of time. A 1985 report by Dr. Nathan Shock, chief of the center, included observations on approximately 650 men and 300 women ranging in age from 17 to 103. In a 1987 article about the study in *The Retired Officer*, magazine writer William Hoffer says:

> Through the years, many of its findings flew in the face of long-accepted myths about old age. For example, the years do not appear to induce personality change, which means that when a previously happy individual develops chronic crankiness it may not be "just a sign of age." More likely, researchers say, it's a sign of Alzheimer's syndrome or psychosis.

So you need not expect to undergo negative changes in your attitudes and emotions—remember, "the mind is the builder"—and, better yet, you can take a more active role in choosing and managing your attitudes. (I talk more about Alzheimer's disease in Chapter 9, on health and diet.)

Table 5
Self-Inventory: Qualities in Others

Part A. Significant Others

Write the names or initials of up to three people with whom you have ongoing, significant relationships:

Part B. Admirable Qualities

Considering your significant others, select the qualities you admire most in one or more of them. Write the initials in the blank next to the qualities. You may add other qualities at the bottom of the columns.

_____ friendly	_____ loving
_____ energetic	_____ objective
_____ patient	_____ serves others
_____ self-confident	_____ joyful
_____ creative	_____ even-tempered
_____ flexible	_____ self-disciplined
_____ enthusiastic	_____ kind
_____ articulate	_____ forgiving
_____ competent	_____ fearless
_____ practical	_____ cooperative
_____ assertive	_____ optimistic
_____	_____
_____	_____

Part C. Irritating Qualities

Considering your significant others, select the qualities that irritate you the most in one or more of them. Write the initials in the blank next to the qualities. You may add other qualities at the bottom of the columns.

_____ aggressive	_____ secretive
_____ forgetful	_____ critical
_____ too talkative	_____ narrow-minded
_____ unemotional	_____ impatient
_____ indecisive	_____ lazy
_____ pessimistic	_____ possessive
_____ self-centered	_____ suspicious
_____ inflexible	_____ vengeful
_____ domineering	_____ uncooperative
_____ unimaginative	_____ boring
_____ stubborn	_____ easily annoyed
_____	_____
_____	_____

YOUR FEELINGS ABOUT OTHERS

The Cayce readings suggest that your work with the relationships in your life may be the most significant effort you can make toward spiritual progress. It is certainly true if you extend the idea, as did one of my elder conversation partners: "It's all in relationships—the relationship to the Father within, to your own spiritual self, to your real world self, to every person and thing around you."

In this section, I concentrate on the attitudes and emotions relating to the people in your life, especially those who are most important to you. The dynamics of your attitudes about others have a unique aspect to them, a boomerang effect. An exercise will get you thinking about your relationships.

GETTING PERSONAL

To focus your thinking, in Part A of the inventory in Table 5, identify up to three people in your life with whom you have your strongest personal relationships—significant others. These will probably be your spouse, close friends, children, or parents.

In Part B select several traits that you most admire in one or more of the people you have identified. Write the initials of the person or persons with the trait in the blank. Feel free to add qualities not listed by writing them in at the bottom of the Part B list.

Then in Part C, select several traits you find most irritating in one or more of your significant others, and write each person's initials in the appropriate blanks. As in Part B, add qualities not listed beside the spaces at the bottom.

One of the most intriguing principles on relationships in the Cayce readings is that the faults you see in others you will also find in yourself—the boomerang effect! Look at Part C in the inventory you just completed. Taken literally, the Cayce principle suggests that you have the irritants in your own personality that you said belonged to others.

Perhaps you either willingly or reluctantly agree that you recognize some of these traits in yourself, but you deny that the rest apply to you. First, try to sort these irritating qualities into three groups:

Faults you still have: Those faults you admit you find in yourself from time to time.

Faults you used to have: Those faults you had earlier in life, but have eliminated or have under control. You are apparently still sensitive to these traits when you see them in others.

Strengths appearing as faults: Those qualities that have two sides to them, according to how they are applied and perceived. For example, if you at one time had a tendency to be wishy-washy about opinions or decisions, your attempts at being more decisive may appear to others like you are inflexible or stubborn. Seeing these faults in others can alert you to the double-edged nature of this quality in yourself. You may have to observe your behavior carefully to recognize this paradoxical trait.

After you have attempted to sort the irritants into these three categories, you may have some left over—traits that do not fit into any of these groups. You feel that they simply do not apply to you. There are two other possible explanations for them:

Faults from previous lives: These are faults you had in one or more past lives that apparently have not carried over into this life. You are ultrasensitive to them because of your past association with them. Seeing such traits in someone else triggers a concern about them, because their patterns are readily accessible to you.

Faults you are concerned about avoiding in yourself: Your sensitivity to these faults may have come about because you sense in yourself a predisposition to them, or a realization that you have subconsciously had to keep a tight control on these attitudes or emotions. Your concern about them in others helps to remind you to steer clear of these undesirable qualities.

So when the Cayce readings say, "Faults in others are first reflected in self" (no. 452–3), the reflection may take any of five forms,
all of which can be instructive. Remember too that finding faults in
others is in itself a fault—one that I encouraged you to do just this
one time. You need not repeat it again!

What about the admirable qualities you see in others close to you?
As with faults, those good qualities you see in others are also in you
in one way or another. You should be able to sort the admirable traits
you have marked in Part B into these groups:

Qualities related to your spiritual ideal: As a step toward
the discovery of your ideals in Chapter 3, you identified several
people you admired and the traits they represented to you. You may
see some of these same traits in your significant others—qualities
that you value and that may be related to your spiritual ideal. These
people may be in your life to serve as models for these admirable
qualities they represent.

Qualities you should work to develop: You draw to yourself
individuals who will help you learn the lessons for which you have
come into the world. They may possess qualities opposite to the
faults you find in yourself. For example, if I tend to be an impatient
person, I notice not only the impatience in others, but also patience,
which can serve as a model for my learning.

Qualities you have: An honest appraisal of yourself will identify admirable traits in your own personality. You will notice these
qualities in others, especially if you are striving to enhance that quality and another person can serve as a model for you.

Perhaps the most important lesson to be learned from observing
others is how much you can find out about yourself. Because the
lessons are for you, you have no reason to share what you observe—
except the nice things:

> If it is impossible to say nice things about a person, keep silent—even
> though what you might say may be true. Remember, there's so much

good in the worst of us that it doesn't behoove the best of us to speak unkindly of any of the rest of us. (no. 3376–1)

ARE YOU FOR GIVING OR FOR TAKING?

Following up on the exercise on relationships, forgiveness may be an appropriate attitude to consider now. One of the elders I spoke with suggests that forgiveness should probably follow thankfulness:

> If I'm not to the point where I can thank God for everything that happens to me, according to what Jesus called the first commandment, then I can work with his second commandment. That brings it down to an individual two-people idea I can work with. And one of the best ways I can express my love for my neighbor is to forgive him or her.

Jesus said that the first commandment was to love your God with all your heart, your soul, your mind, and your strength. One application of this commandment implicit in the Cayce readings is to thank God for whatever happens in your life, both pleasurable and painful. Nothing that happens is really bad. You may not understand at the time, however, how it is good, and in fact, that understanding may never come.

Occasionally I can say, "Thank you, God!" for some of the unwanted occurrences in my life—if not immediately, then soon afterward. For example, when I realized after a recent fall that something was wrong with my wrist, my emotions—anger at my clumsiness, helplessness at my condition, resentment toward our houseful of guests—would have been lessened or even avoided if I had expressed my thanks to God for the opportunities this was bringing me. I was able to do that about two days after the injury, and my perceptions changed accordingly. I began looking for the lessons, for the benefits, and I found them. The very rapid healing that followed is certainly partly attributable to that acceptance and understanding, as well as to the healing prayers and laying on of hands that I accepted from others. Perhaps my experience on this occasion will help me remember to be thankful more quickly on another occasion. (And thank you, God, but I don't need to be tested on that right now!)

If that approach to thankfulness is too difficult to accept and carry out, then consider what Jesus called the second commandment: "Love your neighbor as yourself." Taken together, the message of these two commandments is that your work with your relationships is the most important work of your life—your relationships with other people as well as your relationship with God.

One of my conversation partners suggested:

> Look at the word *forgiveness*. It says I am either "for giving" or I am "for taking"—the only two conditions there are. On the one hand, I am *for giving* something to this relationship, regardless of what the other person has done. Or, on the other hand, I am *for taking* something from this relationship—something for my bruised ego.

As you grow older—and especially as you appraise your life and try to verify its integrity, in the sense Erik Erikson defined it—you review significant events and relationships. Erikson reports in *Vital Involvement in Old Age* that his elder informants described both themselves and their aged contemporaries as "more tolerant, more patient, more open-minded, more understanding, more compassionate, and less critical than they were in younger years." Yet you may recall earlier feelings of hurt, betrayal, resentment, and misplaced trust and affection still associated with individuals. And late in life, you may still be struggling with such feelings about someone.

You can choose an attitude of forgiveness to eliminate the gnawing, destructive influence those negative attitudes and emotions have on you physically, mentally, and spiritually. The following forgiveness process, referred to as the forty-day prayer, was created by Everett Irion, a man who has spent more than twenty-five years working with the Cayce readings. This process, based on his understanding of the teachings of Jesus and the Cayce readings philosophy, is designed to help you release your unfavorable attitudes by replacing them not only with forgiveness, but also with thankfulness for the experience the other person has given you. Many people who have tried this approach have had remarkable results.

The heart of the process is two short, almost identical prayers—one directed to the other person and one to yourself. The process is the same whether the other person is living or dead.

In directing both prayers, Irion suggests using a middle name because you associate it less with the person and your prior interactions with him or her. Let's say my experience was with Lloyd William Smith, whom I always refer to as Lloyd, and my full name is Richard Oscar Peterson, usually referred to as Richard. Irion suggests the following wording:

> William, I am praying to you. Thank you, William, for doing to me all that you have done. Forgive me, William, for doing all that I have done to you.
>
> Oscar, I am praying to you. Thank you, Oscar, for doing to me all that you have done. Forgive me, Oscar, for doing all that I have done to you.

According to Irion, the prayers should continue every day for forty days. Missing a day means going back to the beginning. The long period of time and the consistency will demonstrate your commitment to the healing process. In a current situation that you consider a crisis, the period can be more concentrated, such as once an hour for forty consecutive hours or even once a minute for forty consecutive minutes. After using the prayer each time, put it and the feelings associated with the other person out of your mind completely, so the prayer can do its work without interference from your desires or expectations. Do not tell the other person what you are doing. If you need help in diverting your attention, try saying, "Thank you, God," as often as you can, even hundreds of times a day.

Irion points out that some people find the process especially difficult because they are praying to someone they have had difficulties with, and they are asking forgiveness when they themselves were wronged. But is this not loving your neighbor as yourself, which is the foundation for this recommended process? The only way to determine if it is effective with the stumbling-stone in *your* relationship is to try it.

THE MANY FACES OF FEAR

Most of your attention so far has been focused on your attitudes—toward yourself, toward others, toward events in your life. Recalling

Cayce's distinction between attitudes and emotions, let's refocus on an emotion that can both save you and destroy you—fear.

If suddenly faced with physical danger, the emotion of fear sends signals to the adrenals to start the flow of adrenaline, raise the heart rate, increase the blood flow to the muscles, elevate the blood sugar, and dilate the pupils, all of which may be helpful if you are in a fight or flight dilemma. People have performed unbelievable feats of heroism as well as of self-preservation because of this automatic reaction. Because physical survival is your most basic impulse, this constructive mechanism stimulated by fear must be considered one of your life-sustaining capabilities.

With the exception of this survival-related fear, however, few will deny that fear can be a debilitating and destructive emotion. The effects of frequent bouts with fear are cumulative and may be physically detrimental. The complex physiological reactions involving adrenaline flow, heart rate, blood flow to the muscles, and blood sugar all help to energize you to take extraordinary physical action, during or after which the physiological processes are normalized. When a survival reaction is inappropriate, however, all those physiological changes still take place but do not serve a useful purpose. Eventually, frequent occurrences of these unneeded physiological reactions can have undesirable effects on physical health.

Because the source of the fear is often unknown, nothing can immobilize you as completely as fear. Older people encounter fear with many different faces—fear of change, fear of embarrassment, fear for personal safety, fear of declining abilities, fear of disability, fear about the unknown future, fear of death.

What begins as a reasonable concern, something to address and resolve, often gets ignored or put off. For example, you have to make a decision about moving to a simpler living environment, although you really don't want to give up your space or your privacy. Anxiety and stress start to build, showing themselves in your headaches and fitful sleep, your impatience with housework. Anger may flare up as your well-meaning offspring ask you what you have looked at in alternative living arrangements. As the decision is postponed, these spiraling attitudes and emotions take the form of unreasonable fear of change and fear of new situations.

According to the Cayce readings, fear begins when there is a discrepancy between your actions and the life ideals you use as your yardstick for evaluating your actions. When you live in a manner consistent with that ideal, you experience harmony and stability. When you choose to ignore your spiritual ideals and respond primarily from a physical or mental level (comfort and independence, for example), you begin to experience disharmony, indecision, and doubt—"the father of fear," according to Cayce. Doubt is the attitude, and fear is the emotion it awakens.

In the example concerning a decision to move, consider a widow whose life ideal is human freedom. She owns and cares for a large house bought when her children were young. Much of the house is unused, and she has minimized her responsibilities by closing most of it off and living in three rooms. On the one hand, she enjoys having the neighborhood children all around her, but on the other hand, she doesn't like their running through her yard and making so much noise. Her own adult children have encouraged her to sell the house and move to an apartment in one of the local retirement communities, and she has looked at what's available. She feels it must be her decision and her children are pushing too hard.

On the surface her attitudes of independence and of wanting her privacy and separate space seem consistent with her spiritual ideal of human freedom, and so she should experience harmony. But at a deeper level, she is actually feeling burdened with the house—its taxes, the yard work, its distance from shopping, the general maintenance of the house, even the responsibilities of being a neighbor to boisterous children. The overall effect is one of constraint rather than one of freedom. Her subconscious sense of restriction is not consistent with her ideal of freedom, even though her ability to make her own decision and use her free will seem to support her need for independence. She appears to be operating more from her mental and physical bases than her spiritual base, and that discrepancy leads to fear.

So how would she recognize the inconsistency between her ideal and her deeper feelings? By the doubts and fears she is experiencing as she continues to live in her house. They are a surer sign of a conflict with her ideal than her conscious knowledge that she is being independent in her way of life as well as in her decision making. According to Cayce, she should start by clarifying her ideal. Then she must look deeply within to identify what she is doing that is contrary to that ideal—an exercise in "know thyself."

Even if she cannot identify where she is inconsistent with her ideal, she can practice several other exercises recommended by Cayce for overcoming fear:

Perform some service for others.
Look for the funny side of every experience.
Meditate and pray.
Visualize herself surrounded by the presence of the Christ, walking and talking with him.
Read the gospel of John, chapters 14 through 17.

The magnitude of an emotion may far exceed any apparent cause. Once fear is aroused, it may lay hold of you as if your life were in danger. According to the Cayce readings, fear may be carried over intact from some traumatic past lifetime where the fight for survival was a daily experience, such as with the early settlers of the American West in crossing the Continental Divide; or where the individual faced a life-threatening event, such as an arrest and trial during the French Revolution; or even where the individual had caused others to fear, such as willing participation in witch ducking during the Salem witch trials. Fear is successfully managed by realigning yourself with your ideal, so that fear is not triggered. Some of the Cayce suggestions just listed are directed toward that realignment.

THE FEARSOME FACE OF DEATH

From childhood on, you have had experiences that may remind you dramatically that you too will someday die—the death of a relative or close friend, your own serious accident or illness, a discussion of death in a religious setting, or the news on television. For some people these encounters feed a growing fear of death, fueled by the opinions of others as well as by their own beliefs and imaginings. As you reach your later years, it is natural that you think about your death more frequently, sometimes in a fearful or pessimistic way. In *Vital Involvement in Old Age*, Erikson reports:

> Most of our informants seem to find themselves, almost involuntarily, thinking about dying and about feeling ill, depressed, and somehow let down. To some extent, these thoughts are integral to old age in our society, reflecting a desperation that confronts all elders. However, most people struggle to counterbalance these associations with thoughts of more optimistic, life-affirming involvement.
>
> At the end of life, we may find that some rudimentary hope has blossomed into a mature faith in being that is closely related to essential wisdom.

When you are able to adopt from the "new eyes" paradigm the promise of survival beyond physical death—your many lives on this Earth plus your between-life experiences in other realms—*death* denotes only a point of transition, an end to only one period of your existence and therefore the beginning of another. Because this view is consistent with your ultimate spiritual ideal of Oneness with God, the conditions for fear no longer exist, according to the Cayce readings.

Especially helpful in overcoming fear of death is the frequent Cayce recommendation to read chapters 14 through 17 in the gospel of John, Jesus' message of reassurance to his disciples at the last meal before his arrest and crucifixion:

> Let not your hearts be troubled: believe in God, believe also in me. In my father's house are many rooms. . . . I go to prepare a place for you. (John 14:1–3)

Here are several quotations from the Cayce readings that can help you accept more gracefully the fact of your eventual death:

> A death in the flesh is a birth into the realm of another experience, to those who have lived in such a manner as not to be bound by earthly ties. This does not mean that it does not have its own experience about the earth, but that it has lived such a *fullness* of life that it must be about its business. (no. 989–2)
>
> For there is not death, to those who love the Lord; only the entering into God's other chamber. . . . It is not the end . . . because we pass

from one room to another, from one consciousness to another. (no. 2282–1)

The death is separation, and thus man hath dreaded same; yet when it has lain aside its phase that maketh [him] afraid, it is but the birth into *opportunities* that—if they are embraced with Him, the *truth, as* thy guide—will bring joy and harmony into thy experience! (no. 1776–1)

CHOOSING AND MANAGING YOUR ATTITUDES

Throughout this chapter, I have said that whatever attitudes you now hold, you can choose to have different attitudes. It's one thing to talk about selecting constructive and loving attitudes, and quite another to build them. The Cayce readings encourage you by reminding you to "begin where you are" (no. 4021–1), and that your progress may seem slow: "little by little, line upon line, precept upon precept" (no. 1742–2).

Remember that what manifests as an attitude in the mental and physical had its beginnings in the spiritual. Therefore attitude management has its foundation in the spiritual building blocks:

First, focus on your ideals:

Reevaluate how consistently you are using your spiritual ideal as a standard for your life. Remember that inconsistency between your ideal and your actions contributes to fear.

Include among your mental and physical ideals several related to attitudes and emotions you are trying to change. For example, if I am trying to eliminate a tendency to be critical, I might have a mental ideal to look for qualities that I can be favorable about, and a physical ideal of speaking positively about a situation or person when I am tempted to be critical.

Bring your ideals into your life on a daily basis, with the help of spiritual disciplines or experiments. Set for yourself a reasonable goal for applying a new attitude or emotion in a tangible way every day, and check yourself every night so that you can applaud your efforts and thus reinforce the new attitude or emotion. You can select an experiment to be carried out every day for a week, or you can set up an experiment designed for the situation you will be participating in that day. For example, while I am overcoming being critical of a particular person, a discipline for one week might be to find one thing every day for which I can compliment the individual.

Work with another person or a small group of people who are also interested in trying to change themselves for the better. Share your concerns about your attitudes and emotions, and ask for their suggestions and insights. Such a group need not have a stated goal of spiritual development, but some that do are using as their focus the Edgar Cayce materials titled *A Search for God*. These *Search for God* study groups meet weekly in homes all over the United States and Canada, and in many other parts of the world.

Use meditation and prayer consistently:

Develop affirmations related to the attitudes and emotions you choose to have. Continuing the example of my overcoming being critical, I might use this affirmation every time I see or think about a person I tend to be critical of: "God is present within her, and I praise and love God" or "Everything about him is as it should be, and I thank God for my experience with him."

Include such affirmations in your daily meditation and prayer, and expand on such ideas in your prayers. Seek guidance for ways of demonstrating your new attitudes and emotions and for overcoming undesirable ones.

Use Irion's forty-day prayer of forgiveness to overcome difficulties with specific individuals.

Work with your dreams:

Before you fall asleep, request a dream with a message to help you understand and manage the attitude or emotion you are working on. Commit yourself to remembering and writing down your dreams. Dream work is especially useful in helping you with attitudes and emotions, because dreams bring messages you do not necessarily expect or even want—messages that are accurate and helpful in self-diagnosis.

No experience is more satisfying than realizing a troublesome or undesirable attitude or emotion is no longer a part of your life. In a small way that release can help you feel tangible progress toward Oneness with God.

7

Knowledge and Abilities: "Old Dogs, New Tricks"

Never *forget, that life and its experiences are only what one puts into same! And unless the activities, the thoughts are* continuously *constructive, and the experience well-balanced, [you]* cannot, will not *fulfill the purpose for which [you] came into the present experience.*
EDGAR CAYCE reading no. 1537–1

THERE'S NO POINT IN hiding the fact that this is a chapter about learning new knowledge and skills in your elder years. We may as well have it out right away. Already I can hear some people saying, "Wait a minute—why would I even want to learn anything new? What's the point at my age? Isn't it time I allow myself to sit back and enjoy life and just go with the flow? Besides, remember the cliché about old dogs and new tricks? And I know from what I hear that my mental abilities aren't what they used to be. That means I can't learn as well now that I'm older, so why should I even try?"

IF I WERE YOUNGER . . .

I'll first address the issue of your mental abilities. When traditional psychological studies compared younger and older people on mental tests, younger people usually seemed to do better than older people. More recently researchers have challenged the methods used to measure mental ability in those earlier studies; usually the methods were tests of logic and abstract reasoning. Using a wider variety of measures, psychologist Gisela Labouvie-Vief of Wayne State University found that older adults do not always think logically (hard to believe)—not because they no longer can, but because they use a more complex approach than younger thinkers (I'll bet you knew it all the time!). As reported by Jack Horn and Jeff Meer in the May 1987 issue of *Psychology Today*, she says that the older thinker "operates within a kind of double reality which is both formal and informal, both logical and psychological."

The Baltimore long-term study of aging mentioned earlier reported that mental performance, on the whole, remains strong at least up to age seventy. Then it may decline, but not uniformly. The decline appears at least partly related to use, in that the mental abilities in which older adults show the greatest decline are those they are least likely to use daily.

These newer research findings do not ignore the fact that some diseases, such as Alzheimer's disease and severe depression, may reduce mental abilities and preclude new learning in the later years. But even among those who experience an extensive decline in intellectual ability, at least 15 percent suffer from conditions that are reversible, sometimes through a simple change, such as switching medication. The great majority of older people need not experience a decline in mental abilities. In a June 1986 article in *Psychology Today*, Jeff Meer summarized current studies this way:

> Evidence is piling up that most of our mental skills remain intact as long as our health does, if we keep mentally and physically active. Much of our fate is in our own hands, with "use it or lose it" as the guiding principle. We are likely to slow down in some ways, but there is

evidence that healthy older people do a number of things better than young people.

BUT WHY NOW?

Maybe you'll grant me the fact that most elders have the mental ability to learn and practice new skills or assimilate new knowledge. But you still say, Why make the effort? Don't I deserve to rest on what I've got? Consider what Meer just said about "use it or lose it," and add to that these findings from recent research:

> Men in their 70's who stay proficient in problem-solving tend to live longer. (From the Baltimore longevity study, as reported by William Hoffer in *The Retired Officer*)
>
> The differences in cognitive abilities between the elderly and the young are smaller for abilities that are frequently used by the older adults. (Reported by Nancy Denney in *The Dynamics of Aging*)
>
> A brain that is continually challenged never stops learning. (Dr. K. Warner Schaie, professor of human development, Pennsylvania State University, as reported by Dudley Lynch in *Modern Maturity*, June–July 1986)
>
> The healthy brain continues to gather information over its lifetime. Brain cells are stimulated by use, with a healthy older person's brain getting bigger with age. (Neurologist Carl Cotman, University of California, Irvine, as reported in the September 1987 *AARP News Bulletin*)

In brief, using your mental abilities not only acts to prevent their decline, but it may strengthen them and cause the brain to keep growing!

As you experience changes in the externals of your life—retirement, relocation, simplification of your way of life, reduced responsibilities—you may find yourself unable to use some of your valued skills and knowledge. For example, most people retired from an occupation in which they were successful have little opportunity to use their specialized skills or to keep up with new ideas and techniques in that field—and may not want to. Whether the occupation is accounting, management, child rearing, data processing, or automobile assembly, many of the skills and much of the knowledge of a career are no longer relevant. As a result, you may find your perspective narrowing, your world getting smaller, and some abilities deteriorating from lack of use. You may call it deserved relaxation and even contentment. The Cayce readings, however, suggest that "life must be a well-balanced life, not lopsided in any manner, to bring contentment—not necessarily be satisfied, for that is to become stagnant" (no. 349–6). Paraphrasing the Cayce quotation at the beginning of this chapter, you get out of life only what you put into it!

Have you ever had an interest in something without having enough time to do much about it? What about now? Gail Sheehy expresses it this way in *Passages:*

> Secondary interests that have been tapped earlier in life can in middle and old age blossom into a serious lifework. Each tap into a new vessel releases in the later years another reservoir of energy. An aspect of life that was dominant and satisfying earlier—the excitement of competing in business or taking care of children, for instance—should not be expected to be forever the mainstay of one's life.

Even if you haven't identified these "secondary interests" in your middle years, you can develop new interests in your later years and learn the required new skills and knowledge to go with them. Later in this chapter, I will help you discover prospective new interests and suggest some ways of cultivating them, including the development of your psychic ability.

How far you get in your new field is immaterial, according to the Cayce readings, because whatever you have started can be carried over to your next life experience. One of my elder conversation partners said:

> I remember a reading in which Edgar Cayce told one elderly man that he might as well take piano lessons, because he'd be that much ahead in the next lifetime. I feel that way too. Any sincere effort is never lost.

Anything we achieve now is going to be helpful forever, so why not go on trying?

Another elder person who worked in Japan for several years told me about his plan to continue studying Japanese:

> I don't know whether I shall ever physically go back to Japan or not. But with this larger understanding of human destiny, my own included, I have just as much reason to continue the study of the Japanese language, because I may need it again—if not in this life, perhaps in another. Furthermore, in some way this can help me, even prepare me, for creative activity here and now. These perspectives on human life are enormous help in encouraging one to keep going—to keep on keeping on!

Finally, consider the fun and satisfaction of learning something new that you choose to learn at your speed and to your standards. After all the years of learning what you had to learn to do your job and to get along in the world, now you can choose to learn something just for the sake of learning it. Let's look at your own vision of your future.

GETTING PERSONAL

In Chapter 1, I asked you what you would like to be doing on your next few decade birthdays, circumstances and resources permitting. Go back to the notes you made at that time.

For each of the years you have written about, identify what special skills, information, or knowledge you would need to have to do what you would like to do. For example, if you would like to be sailing a schooner in the Caribbean, have you ever learned to sail? Do you know how to read navigational charts? Or if one of your visions is to take a cruise or visit Europe or China, wouldn't your trip be more enjoyable if you learned about some of the places you would like to visit? You get the idea.

Take time now to make a list of the special skills and knowledge that would help bring about what you visualize for yourself in the decades ahead.

If your "future vision" doesn't include any experiences requiring new skills or knowledge, you may get some ideas from the suggestions in the next section of this chapter.

CHOOSING THE RIGHT "NEW TRICK"

The Cayce reading that opened this chapter reminds you of the need to live a balanced life if you seek contentment. Balance includes your attention to all three aspects of your life—the physical, the mental, and the spiritual. As you consider taking up new interests in your later years, you can choose them with a secondary goal of bringing more balance into your life. The suggestions that follow are grouped according to whether they are predominantly physical, mental, or spiritual. They include ideas stimulated by the Cayce readings, by recent news articles, and by the experiences of elders with whom I spoke. These suggestions may in turn trigger ideas reflecting your own environment and experience.

New Physical Interests

Whole Body Activities

Walking, preferably in natural settings; adds the spiritual benefits of spending time in nature that the Cayce readings identify. Many recent books and a magazine called *Walking* can add to the enjoyment and benefit of this activity.

Swimming, a gentle way to involve the whole body, with low strain on bones and joints, which are buoyed by the water. Many swimming centers, such as the YMCA, schedule sessions for the adult learner and some have aquatic programs for those with limited mobility. There are even swimming programs for people who have always hated the water.

Yoga, especially the simpler disciplines and postures. Yoga classes are available in many localities, but you may prefer learning on your own from a guide such as *Easy Does It Yoga for Older People*, by Alice Christensen and David Rankin.

Olympics-type competition geared to the older adult. Some people are better able to sustain their interest in learning and practicing physical skills when competition is involved. The U.S. Masters Swimming program, for example, provides local, regional, and national meets and awards, with competitors divided by five-year age brackets (for example, those sixty to sixty-four compete with one another). The National Senior Olympics program is designed for competitors fifty-five and older. A recent regional meet called the Golden Olympics included swimming, golf, discus, shot put, basketball free throws, croquet, running, softball hit and throw, doubles tennis, table tennis, billiards, bridge, horseshoes, bowling, fly casting, and archery—and that wasn't the entire list. Take your choice or become a many-skilled Olympian.

Crafts and Other Technical Skills

Working with wood, metal, plastic, fabric, or yarn to create objects. If past occupations have been highly mental in their activity, the later years may provide the time for restoring a balance—for learning crafts and creating articles both decorative and useful in the product, as well as satisfying in the production. Among the many crafts available, probably several fit both your physical capabilities and your pocketbook. Walking through a large crafts department or store will present possibilities you may never have considered before.

Raising flowers, herbs, or other plants, either indoors or outdoors. Learning and working with the laws—and whims—of nature is another way to follow the Cayce recommendations for spending time in natural settings with living plants. Consider specializing in a single flower and its many varieties. Or learn how to grow and use herbs in cooking, in decoration, and in health remedies such as suggested in many of the Cayce readings. The study and use of herbs is an activity that has physical, mental, and spiritual values.

Interpersonal Relationship Skills (has both physical and mental aspects)

Bringing new skills to an existing relationship. Many relationships, including marriages, can use new vitality in the elder years. This can come about if both people take up a new skill or activity together, whether physical (such as dancing), mental (such as learning a foreign language), or spiritual (such as meditation). New values may also be added to a relationship by improving interpersonal communication, by discovering sources of annoyance that each finds in the other and replacing them with sources of enjoyment, and, if the relationship has included sexual activity, by finding new ways of enjoying one another's sexuality.

Building new relationships. Set a goal to make at least one new friend and to build and nurture a friendship. Plan to put yourself in situations where you will meet new people in a way comfortable for you. Make the effort to learn names and other personal details, carry on a meaningful conversation, and listen well. If you're out of practice or shy, consider classes or books that help you develop some of these interpersonal skills.

New Mental Interests

Education through programs of formal instruction, such as public schools, colleges, or adult education institutes. Data from the Center for Education Statistics show that the number of people sixty-five or older enrolled in adult education of all kinds increased from 765,000 in 1981 to 866,000 in 1984, and the number continues to increase rapidly from year to year. It is not unusual to see elders receiving undergraduate or graduate degrees at a college graduation ceremony. In 1987 the LaFarge Lifelong Learning Institute was presented with the first American Association of Retired Persons (AARP) award for leadership in providing opportunities for people to learn in their later years. The Milwaukee-based institute offers more than one hundred courses in twelve-week semesters to anyone fifty years of age or older. At the ceremony John Denning, the AARP president at the time, said that, "Education can be one of the greatest means of empowering people at any age and should continue throughout an entire lifetime." The concept of empowerment during a period when many people feel increasingly powerless could be a reason in itself for new learning.

Elderhostel provides a rich variety of educational experiences for adults sixty years old and older "who want to continue to expand their horizons and to develop new interests and enthusiasms," according to the Elderhostel catalog. Its programs are usually one week long, scheduled year round at more than 1200 colleges and other educational facilities in all fifty states and Canada, with longer programs in countries all over the world. In 1988 more than 165,000 elders were enrolled in these programs—up from 6000 in 1982.

Special projects for learning are suggested by two notable elders, Harmon Bro and Malcolm Cowley. From his years working with Edgar Cayce, Bro identified several activity "tracks" that Cayce used in his own life to take tangible steps toward building a better world. Two of those tracks illustrate Bro's idea:

Pick one people other than your own—a race, religious sect, or national group, for example—and become informed on it, not only by reading the best books and articles about that people, but by getting into its history, its politics, its literature, and its religious writings.

Pick one modern social problem and become an informed resource on it, not only by reading, but by getting out to see what people are doing to solve the problem. For example,

what is going on in your area to help the elderly homeless or
poor?

Bro recommends not merely a passive mental learning, but one
that eventually could lead you into activities that contribute
to healing the world.

In his *View from Eighty*, Malcolm Cowley says,

> Poet or housewife, businessman or teacher, every old person needs
> a work project if he wants to keep himself alive. . . . It should be
> big enough to demand his best efforts, yet not so big as to dis-
> hearten him and let him fall back into apathy. . . . One project
> among many . . . that tempts me and might be tempting to others,
> is trying to find a shape or pattern in our lives. There are such pat-
> terns, I believe, even if they are hard to discern.

Metaphysics and esoteric knowledge, such as that found in the
Cayce readings. One approach is to learn more about the readings themselves and the philosophy presented in them through
books and conferences on the material, and through study of
the readings themselves. Another approach is to concentrate on
specific topics within the readings, such as diet, dreams, reincarnation, and the Edgar Cayce health remedies. Still another
approach is to read other sources on Cayce-related subjects,
such as gemstones, the story of Jesus and those around him,
astrology, and the mysteries of ancient Egypt and Atlantis.

Personal computer skills, ranging from simple word processing
capabilities to advanced programming. The microcomputer is
becoming more accessible to everyone, both in price and in
availability without ownership. For example, some public li-
braries now have computers available for patrons to learn on
and use in a supervised setting. Courses in fundamental computer skills are popular in adult education programs, and many
bookstores carry well-written guides on everything from creating your own video games to programming your income tax
records and returns. And as with other special activities, you
may focus more on the processes—the learning, the problem
solving, the development of a simple application—than on the
products themselves.

Puzzles and mental aerobics that challenge and stretch your cognitive and problem-solving skills. When my father retired at sixty-five, I gave him a pencil and clipboard and a subscription to a puzzle magazine, although he was not a "puzzler," as I was. At ninety-two, he subscribes to two puzzle magazines and buys others off the rack in order to find enough of his favorite cryptographic puzzles. Although his eyesight often requires him to bring the page up close to his eyes or use a large magnifier, he spends pleasurable hours every day on his puzzles. He credits them for having kept his mind active these past twenty-seven years. The June–July 1986 issue of *Modern Maturity*, the bimonthly magazine of the AARP, carried a page of "mind aerobics" by Dudley Lynch, a "brain trainer." One of his recommendations is to become addicted to the mental challenge of crossword puzzles and to spatial- and manual-skill games, because they "put the brain's chemical and electrical mechanisms through their paces." Lynch suggests exercises that allow you to sample your psychic ability. For example, he proposes that you practice foretelling the future to "put your forward-thinking frontal lobes to work," and to imagine yourself doing a task before you do it, thus "exercising your right brain hemisphere's visualizing apparatus."

New Spiritual Interests

Self-analysis and spiritual study, taking forms such as renewed interest in a traditional religion; application of the spiritual building blocks of life ideals and purpose, meditation, prayer, and dreams; or participation in a *Search for God* study group or a group studying *A Course in Miracles* or other spiritual material. Malcolm Cowley's personal project fits this category. The Cayce readings frequently recommend the study of chapters 14 through 17 of John's gospel as a guide to self-knowledge and spiritual development; several of these readings are directed to elders. One of the simplest and yet most helpful techniques of self-analysis involves keeping a personal journal, oriented toward the expression of ideas, feelings, dreams, and concerns of the inner life. Ira Progoff's book *At a Journal Workshop* is a classic introduction to the use of the intensive journal.

Developing intuition and psychic abilities. According to the Cayce readings, intuition taps into available spiritual forces while you are conscious, and dreams tap those forces while you are unconscious. In your peak activity years, distracting influences may have prevented you from experiencing your intuition fully, although you can probably remember having had hunches or sudden inspirations. In your later years, you have fewer distractions and more time to learn how to awaken and sense your intuition, plus a wide range of knowledge and experience for intuition to tie into. This is such an intriguing possibility for new learning by elders that the next section of this chapter is devoted to it.

DEVELOPING INTUITION AND PSYCHIC ABILITY

In the Cayce readings the words *psychic* and *intuitive* are used almost interchangeably. In everyday speech, however, *intuitive* is a more acceptable word than *psychic* for the sudden insight or new idea that seems to appear from nowhere. Everyone has the potential for being psychic, because everyone has access to the knowledge and resources from the Creative Forces also called God. In fact, children often demonstrate psychic ability until they learn that information received intuitively is often unacceptable to the logical adults around them. Then suppression begins and natural psychic ability may all but disappear.

Now, much later in life, you may want to begin to recognize the naturalness of your original ability and allow yourself to redevelop the skill. By definition the process is not logical, and logic has been a prized quality in our Western culture, so you have to learn to go counter to much of your past learning. But the results you can get with a sincere effort at being open to psychic sources is worth the effort.

The psychic process has as its foundation the building blocks presented in this book. In a sense this whole book is designed to enhance your psychic ability. In this section I present a summary of the primary principles and steps of the process as they appear in the Cayce material.

The outline of the psychic process is similar to the process of meditation detailed in Chapter 4. The stages are preparation and attunement, awareness and receptivity, and evaluation and application.

Stage One: Preparation and Attunement for Intuition

The stage of preparation and attunement is one of habitual practice, with the following activities being carried out on a daily basis:

Physical preparation includes getting sufficient physical exercise, keeping to a healthy diet, and maintaining correct body alignment through periodic spinal adjustments. Another physical activity is spending time in nature, to take advantage of the affinity between nature and the natural process of intuition.

Mental preparation includes Bible study, because the readings suggest it is a guide to spiritual growth as well as an account of humanity's efforts to achieve Oneness with God. Essential to the psychic process is the management of your attitudes and emotions, replacing doubt and fear (which block intuition) with faith, hope, trust, and belief (which facilitate intuition).

The key to spiritual preparation for intuition is, not surprisingly, attunement to your spiritual ideal and life purpose. This should include an assessment of why you want to enhance your psychic abilities, and how you will use your intuition if it is more highly developed. Your motivation must be aligned with your spiritual purpose before you can tap the Universal Source. Psychic ability will also be greatly facilitated by regular application of the other spiritual building blocks of meditation, prayer, and dream work. Participation in a spiritual growth group is also recommended. The twenty-four lessons in *A Search for God*, the texts used in weekly study groups, were prepared with the assistance of a special series of Cayce readings (the 262 series) and are essential steps for developing psychic ability through spiritual development.

Stage Two: Awareness and Receptivity for Intuition

Becoming aware of and receptive to your intuition means, paradoxically, following a logical set of techniques and steps for facilitating a
phenomenon that defies logic. The following activities are suggested
by the Cayce readings or those who have worked on enhancing
psychic ability:

Participate in activities that stretch your imagination and stimulate your creativity. Strengthening imagination is a route to intuition
because, according to the readings, "anyone with great imagination,
of course, is intuitive" (no. 1744–1).

Pay attention to thoughts and impressions you get in the hypnagogic state, as you are falling asleep or waking up. The conscious and
subconscious minds are battling for dominance during this state, and
information from the subconscious mind often flows freely into the
conscious mind. The subconscious may hold information obtained
from the Universal Sources, so your thoughts at such times may include psychically received information.

Begin to trust your inner promptings, even when they seem illog-
ical. Beginning cautiously with small matters, act on some of your
hunches or intuitive flashes. Even if you do not take action, record
them for future review and evaluation. You will know whether you
are truly tuned in by the results of your actions or by looking back at
your information in light of later events. As you begin to trust your
intuition, also let go of your expectations.

Conduct your own psychic experiments. For example, before
going to an unfamiliar place—a house, a room, a city—visualize it.
Or before something occurs, such as a party or a trip, picture what it
will be like when it is happening, see some of the events that will take
place. Jot down a description or a sketch of what you visualize or
anticipate. Or plan with someone else to send a message or image
psychically one to the other at a specific time.

Determine your own method for receiving psychic information.
Some people experience intuition directly and clearly, that is, information is received in words either heard or read or in images perceived; little or no interpretation is needed. Some people experience

intuition primarily through emotional reactions during meditation or at other times of attunement, and some get a clear sense of emotions in others, especially those with whom they have a close relationship. (One of the cautions expressed in the Cayce readings is to avoid making hasty judgments about others based on intuitive feelings.) Some people receive information that comes to the surface only when they begin to express themselves through art, music, dance, writing, or other forms of creative expression. Some people experience intuition through events in their lives, through the special kind of meaningful coincidence that Carl Jung called synchronicity.

As you begin to work with intuition, other techniques and approaches will emerge. The title I have given this stage—awareness and receptivity—is a reminder that those are the essential attitudes of psychic ability.

Stage Three: Evaluation and Application of Intuitive Information

If information received psychically is objective and factual, then it can be evaluated on the basis of its resemblance to reality. For example, if you visualize a home you are about to visit for the first time, the images you receive can be readily evaluated against what you see when you arrive.

If psychically received information cannot be objectively checked, as in the case of guidance about a decision or problem, evaluation is more difficult. Here are some questions you can ask about such information:

Is the information helpful and hopeful?
Is it consistent with my ideals?
Does it ring true? Does it feel right?
Does it help me to stretch, to discover new aspects of life?
Does it encourage me toward the best I know to do and be?
Does it answer questions I didn't ask but needed answered?
Does it give me specific things I can apply?

These criteria all tend to confirm information that is positive, constructive, or growth-directed, and tend to deny whatever is negative, destructive, or stagnant. Using such criteria provides built-in protection for your psychic development.

The only sure way to evaluate nonobjective information received intuitively is to apply it and evaluate the results. As with meditation and dreams, the psychic process has not ended until application is begun. The Cayce readings warn against repeatedly repressing or denying intuitive impressions, suggesting that inner turmoil and stress will result. Also, without application and follow-through, your psychic ability will not develop, just as it may have faded from your repertoire of capabilities when, as a child, you began to ignore it.

This gives you enough to start developing your psychic ability. When you have put these ideas into action, your intuition will guide you on what to do next.

GETTING PERSONAL

It's time for a personal commitment to some new activity of learning and skill-stretching. With the Cayce injunction in mind to move "step by step, precept by precept," start small, but commit yourself to begin a new activity on a regular basis—daily? weekly?—and to continue it for a reasonable period of time—several weeks? several months?

Look back at the earlier "Getting Personal" exercise in this chapter. Can you select something from that to get started on? Also review the balance of physical, mental, and spiritual priorities in your life and consider learning something that will bring you more into balance. Finally, scan the list of new physical, mental, and spiritual activities suggested in this chapter to see if anything comes to the forefront for you.

Make a list of alternatives, if you have several, and evaluate them in terms of time required, cost, accessibility, estimated period needed to feel some progress or accomplishment, and so on. From these considerations, select a new learning activity. Because a written agreement is likely to be more of a commitment than a mental note, write a simple contract with yourself about your commitment. This can include a date by which you agree to begin your learning, and a date by which you will evaluate your progress and your choice of activity. If you really need some extra motivation, specify a reward for yourself when you reach a specific goal (such as make one craft project, have one new friend, complete one course, or finish reading one book).

———————————

Whatever you choose to learn, by all means, also choose to relax and enjoy the learning. Consider it an investment in your future as well as a confirmation of your present. Feel your abilities and your knowledge being stimulated and extended "here a little, there a little." Remember, points are given just for trying.

8

Memory: Use It or Lose It!

To acknowledge that the memory is poor is to say you don't think much!

EDGAR CAYCE reading no. 69–2

A CONCERN THAT NAGS many elders today was expressed in these questions asked of Edgar Cayce:

Why is it difficult for me to remember? (no. 69–2)

How may my memory and power of concentration be improved? (no. 1152–2)

Are there any ways that I can improve my memory, particularly for people, their faces, names, and facts pertaining to them? (no. 261–7)

What causes, and what should be done to overcome, unsatisfactory memory? (no. 2783–1)

I recently experienced memory lapses on several occasions within a few days of one another. None of them was significant—I went to where I keep my tools, but couldn't remember what I was there for; I needed to buy something on my next trip to the supermarket, but forgot it before I could write it down; I could not recall the author of the book I had just been reading; and so on. After a number of these incidents, I realized I was becoming anxious about my memory. Aware that "the mind is the builder," I knew I needed to stop the anxiety and forestall fear. As I observed myself after that, I realized that when I paid more attention to what I was doing, I was not forgetful. My problem was not memory, but concentration—keeping focused on what I was doing, living in the now.

You may have encountered elders with severe memory impairment. Some may even have Alzheimer's disease, which usually begins with losses in memory and cognitive skills. Your direct experiences and observations make lasting impressions, and you may have begun to associate old age with poor memory. When you couple that association with your own momentary forgetfulness, you may have drawn hasty and incorrect conclusions about your own memory.

Recent research indicates that the normal, healthy older person does not experience a decline in memory. In Meer's June 1986 *Psychology Today* article, psychologist Ilene Siegler of Duke University Medical Center makes this refreshing observation:

> As we get older, old age gets blamed for problems that may have existed all along. A 35-year-old who forgets his hat is forgetful, but if the same thing happens to Grandpa we start wondering if his mind is going.

Forgetfulness can be caused by incorrect medication, depression, stress, insufficient sleep, distractability, and other correctible physical and mental problems. The treatment of memory loss is the subject of Siegfried Kra's book *Aging Myths: Reversible Causes of Mind and Memory Loss*. And even with more severe losses that typify dementia, Dr. James Foley, a neurologist at the Case Western Reserve University School of Medicine, estimated recently that some improvement is possible with 75 percent of all those who come to his office exhibiting confused behavior (reported in the October 1987 *AARP News Bulletin*).

Working under a grant from the National Institute on Aging, Willard Rogers and Regula Herring of the University of Michigan compared the accuracy of memory for factual information among three age groups: younger than age sixty, ages sixty through sixty-nine, and ages seventy and older. As reported in a 1987 article by Susan Landers in *Monitor*, those sixty and older were the most accurate on most of the facts requested, with no consistent differences between the two older groups. Those seventy and older tended to overestimate the distance from home to the nearest drugstore, and younger people tended to underestimate it—a perception more than a memory, and one probably affected by the ease of getting around.

The Edgar Cayce readings identify several causes for memory loss in answer to questions such as those that began this chapter:

Forgetting may result if thought is self-centered, or if something within a person (an inner consciousness) rebels.

Lack of concentration and uncoordinated mental reactions may result from overtaxing or overstraining the body, and from "distress between the coordinations of the cerebrospinal and sympathetic [nervous] systems" of the body (no. 2771–2). On the other hand, the mind of an active, healthy person is not overburdened with memory activity.

Inability to recall may result from poor circulation, which in turn allows toxic forces to build up in the body and affect mental reactions.

Critical, destructive, and unproductive attitudes may inhibit memory.

Later in this chapter I present suggestions from the Cayce readings for improving memory and concentration.

WHAT IS THIS THING CALLED MEMORY?

According to a theoretical model of memory developed by psychologist Marcia Johnson of Princeton University, as outlined in an article by Laurie Denton in *Monitor* in 1987, memory is

a complex set of interacting subsystems, serving different functions and represented by different neural structures. These subsystems develop at different rates and may be differentially susceptible to disruption caused by aging, Alzheimer's disease, drug or alcohol use, amnesias and delusional syndromes.

Her theory proposes three memory subsystems—sensory, perceptual, and reflective. The sensory subsystem records sense cues of which you are often unaware, such as brightness, place, and direction of movement. The perceptual subsystem records cues from external objects in relation to each other, such as a book on a table or two people in an automobile. Together the sensory and perceptual subsystems hold your externally generated memories. In contrast, the reflective subsystem records active thinking, judging, and comparing—internally generated memories, such as ideas retained from this book.

If the reflective subsystem becomes blocked—by trauma or disease, for example—the record of the past is also blocked, resulting in amnesia, according to Johnson's theory. If the reflective subsystem is overworked, delusions may result. So in a sense, Johnson says, memory is balanced between amnesia and delusion. If you analyze the mental behavior of some victims of Alzheimer's disease or other forms of senility, you see evidence of both amnesia and delusions.

According to Cayce, however, memory is never really lost, even in the case of amnesia. It is merely inaccessible until a blockage is removed, as Johnson implies in her model. Also, brain surgery has demonstrated that long-forgotten memories can be brought to the conscious mind when the outer cortex of the brain is stimulated electrically.

The Cayce readings imply other complexities and subtleties in the operation of memory. For example, memory is defined as "the exercising of the inner self as related to thought" (no. 69–2), and it is affected by "the vibration that has to do with the sensory system and the sympathetic nerve system" (no. 287–3) and by toxic substances that build up in a sluggish circulatory system, especially in the lymph glands and the ganglia along the spinal system.

The effects of aging vary according to how much has to be retrieved from memory and at what level of memory the information resides. Try this short exercise as an introduction to levels of memory:

GETTING PERSONAL

1. Make a list of seven to ten items you might shop for or errands you might run in the next few days.

    Look the completed list over with the intention of remembering it. Then set it aside for now.

2. In your telephone directory look up the number for a friend or a business for which you do not know the number. Commit the number to memory, and then, without taking the telephone off the hook, dial the number. Repeat this for two other numbers, one at a time. If necessary, look numbers up a second time to check yourself.

    How would you rate your memory for these numbers on a scale from 1 to 10, with 10 being fast and accurate?

3. Remember your early school experiences and recall the names of as many of your teachers as you can. Try to picture each teacher in your mind. Write down the name of each one recalled.

    On a scale from 1 to 10 (10 being several teachers immediately recalled and pictured), how do you think you did?

4. Without looking at the list you made (in no. 1 above) of things to buy or do, write down as many of the items as you can.

    Comparing your remembered list with the original list, how would you rate your degree of recall on a scale from 1 to 10, with 10 as all items recalled quickly and accurately?

You were experiencing short-term (number 2), long-term (number 3), and intermediate-term (number 4) memory in a *recall* mode. If you had been asked to look at a list of names or a set of pictures from which to identify former teachers, you would have been responding in a *recognition* mode for long-term memory.

It is not surprising if you found you were not equally skilled with all three levels of memory. This is what research says about them:

Long-term memory is least affected by age. In fact, some research indicates that older people may be more efficient and accurate in scanning their long-term memory than younger people, apparently becoming more efficient because of their greater accumulation of memories. The strength of long-term memory in older adults shows up in their fascination with reminiscence, a fascination sometimes greeted with dismay by younger companions. Considering your long-term memory as reflected in the preceding exercise, would you have done any better ten, fifteen, or twenty-five years ago? Perhaps not, if you had never tried to remember your teachers' names or faces.

Intermediate-term memory includes, for example, recalling a list of items to do or steps to take, and remembering facts and meanings from recent reading, viewing, or hearing. Some decline in this level of memory is evident among many elders, but the degree of loss varies widely according to the type of material, with whom they are compared, the frequency of demand on the memory, the amount of time available to recall, and the criteria used to judge the final expression of the memory. Older adults may require more time to recall and be more forgetful under time pressure (tell me about it!). What they retrieve may be more in terms of meanings than in terms of exact words, in contrast to young people, who more typically remember the words.

Short-term memory is involved when you look up a telephone number and then dial it immediately from memory, or look up an address and then write it down without copying it. The Baltimore aging study indicates that this type of material may be remembered more slowly by older people, but is remembered as completely as by younger people. That is, if you have developed your ability for short-term memory—and it is a skill that can be enhanced with practice—you should expect to retain that skill as long as you continue to exercise it, although it may take you a little longer than younger people.

So how did you do at each of these levels of memory? Although you can certainly feel good about your memory if your ratings were high, don't be too hard on yourself if your ratings were low. You may simply not be in the habit of exercising your memory in these ways.

The Cayce quotation at the beginning of this chapter might be restated as the cliché of the chapter title: "Use it or lose it!" This curt warning is confirmed by much of the recent research and experience on memory and aging. Both the Cayce material and the research go further to say that, even when memory skills have declined from lack of use, they can be redeveloped and sharpened. The recommendations in the next section are based on the information in the research, as well as on suggestions in the Cayce material.

TECHNIQUES FOR IMPROVING MEMORY AND CONCENTRATION

Any effort you make to prevent memory decline or to improve memory will be more effective if you apply those efforts at the spiritual and physical levels, as well as at the mental level. A Cayce reading referring to memory says

> For it must come first in spirit, then in mind, then materialize. For it is the natural law. (no. 2783–1)

Working With the Spiritual

The readings emphasize two of the spiritual building blocks as fundamental to memory retention and improvement. First, be certain about your ideals and your life's purpose. If your behavior is in any way at odds with your ideals, you can expect a detrimental effect on memory—one type of internal rebellion, mentioned earlier as a cause of memory problems.

The ability to concentrate for remembering as well as for other purposes can be significantly improved through the spiritual building block of meditation and prayer. Meditation itself requires concentration and, according to Cayce, its regular practice with a focus on the ideal will strengthen the powers of concentration and memory.

Based in the spiritual realm as well as in the mental are the suggestions made in the readings to set your personality self aside, to lose yourself in what is being done, especially for others, to align yourself with love. As a consequence, memory and concentration will improve.

Working With the Physical

Two physical treatments that may have positive effects on memory and concentration are massage and spinal adjustment; both improve the flow of energy systems in the body. The massage must be one that releases toxins, especially those built up in the lymph glands and certain muscle groups, and move them so they are first dissipated and then eliminated. The massage should give special attention to the ganglia along the spine. Then spinal adjustment by a qualified practitioner can unblock the flow in the circulation through the nerves and the blood system. Both massage and spinal adjustments can also relieve physical tensions and stresses that inhibit memory and concentration. The Cayce readings often provide instructions to their subjects about the specific manner of massage and spinal adjustment, clearly suggesting that not just any massage or spinal treatment would have the anticipated results.

Cayce mentions the head and neck exercise described in Chapter 4 as an aid in concentrated mental activity. Such activity draws upon nervous energy that sometimes gets localized in the upper cervical area through the neck and between the shoulders. According to Cayce, doing the head and neck exercise and drinking water can "recharge the battery force" of the body (no. 1554–4).

Some Cayce readings suggest memory training just before and after sleeping. Study and read material you want to remember just before sleeping, and recall it when you wake up. A presleep suggestion to the mind that you will remember what you need to know makes your intent and commitment clearer. This same exercise can also be carried out before and after meditation.

One simple and direct instruction is, "Apply daily what ye desire to remember, and ye will grow in memory" (no. 2783–1). When you put into application the knowledge and skills you acquire, you are better able to remember them.

Finally, the readings frequently remind you that a healthy body through proper diet and exercise is essential for all your systems, including your mental system. A sluggish body means a sluggish mind, to paraphrase many Cayce references.

Working With the Mental

Because both physical and mental strain depress the memory function, you must be aware of your stress threshold and keep stress under control—for reasons that go beyond memory improvement. Cayce mentions several times the disruption of memory by attitudes and emotions—"animosities," allowing yourself "to get riled," being "at variance with the will" of others, rebuking others. One reading says that forgetfulness comes from an attitude of self-centeredness. Another reading says that mental activities will be more effective if you adopt a "positive, sympathetic, lovable, even manner." The mental building block of managing your attitudes and emotions is important in protecting and enhancing your memory.

In his responses to questions about memory improvement techniques, Cayce suggests "practice," "any course of memory tests," "mental training by association of ideas," and emphasis on "that which is creative." The memory training exercises in the next section incorporate those general hints with concepts and ideas from other sources.

EXERCISES FOR STRENGTHENING MEMORY

This section presents a variety of exercises recommended both for preventing memory decline and for improving memory. The activities are grouped by level of memory—short-term, intermediate-term, or long-term—and by type of memory—recognition or recall.

The exercises illustrate the kinds of experiences that can be helpful in reinforcing and stretching your memory. As you try these you may identify activities more appropriate to your own needs and interests. At the end of the chapter is a "Getting Personal" section that asks you to select exercises for practice, so read the list with the intent of making selections.

Short-Term Recall Exercises

1. *Telephone number/address recall:* Repeat exercise number 2 in the preceding "Getting Personal" section, but do it ten times or more, looking up a different unknown number each time. Or do a similar lookup of ten or more unfamiliar addresses in your telephone directory or address book, and commit them to memory long enough to write them down. Even within a span of ten to fifteen repetitions, you may see an improvement in your skill.

2. *Reading recall:* This exercise combines short-term recall with comprehension. Select an article you have not read from a newspaper or magazine, or a chapter from a nonfiction book. Read one or more paragraphs at a time and then immediately write a brief summary of main points, or words or phrases that stick in your mind. Continue reading, recalling, and writing for a total of five or more segments. If you finish an article, write a brief summary of the whole piece.

Intermediate-Term Recall Exercises

3. *List recall:* Repeat the list exercise from the preceding "Getting Personal" section several times with different kinds of lists. Also practice making a shopping or errand list, and then doing the shopping or errands without the list.

4. *Steps/recipe recall:* Select a process with several steps, such as a recipe or the procedure for a small craft project. Review the process by reading the instructions, visualizing the steps and activities in your mind. Then set it aside while you carry out the activity. Go back and check your recipe or procedure to verify that you have done everything correctly.

5. *Remembering people at a gathering:* Next time you go to a

party, a committee meeting, or a church supper where you meet people you don't know, practice remembering names and other details about new people, including any feelings you have about them. Be sure you understand each new name when you hear it or see it. When introduced, repeat it to the person. Use it at least twice during the gathering. Use the name in talking to the individual or about the individual to someone else. As other details are learned about the person—family, occupation, hobbies, likes and dislikes—try to associate the details with something in the name or the appearance of the person. After the event write down names, descriptions, feelings, and other details about as many people as you can recall. Cayce suggests that if you're good at facts or figures, for example, but not at names, faces, or abilities, associate the names and faces with facts or figures about the people.

6. *Reading comprehension and recall:* Select an article or short story of several pages for reading and remembering. Read the material all the way through without taking notes. Then set it aside and summarize the main points of the article or the plot of the story. Variation: Read the article or story just before going to sleep. Instruct your mind that you will remember a summary of the material when you wake up. Sleep. When you wake up, recall the main points or the plot and any feelings you had about the material.

Long-term Recognition and Recall Exercises

7. *Object recognition and information recall:* Stand in the middle of a room and name objects you see in the room as quickly as you can. Include descriptive details, such as colors or types—an Indian rug of red, brown, gold, and blue; a bookshelf with an encyclopedia set, novels, biographies, books on healing; and so on. Variation: If you have a drawer of kitchen implements or a workbench of assorted tools, try the same exercise, naming each item as quickly as you can and stating

what it is used for. (This may sound too simple to give you any memory exercise; I urge you to try it.)

8. *People recognition and recall:* Gather several photographs of relatives, friends, and acquaintances. Name everyone in the pictures, state where they are now if you know, their relationship to you, your feelings about each of them. Variation: Use pictures of celebrities or other people you recognize, recalling names and other details you know.

9. *Musical recognition and recall:* As you listen to a radio program of continuous music you enjoy, recall names of songs or compositions, composers, and performers. Variation: Recall the words to familiar songs.

10. *Autobiographical recall:* Select a period of your life, such as grade school, military service, or your first home after your marriage. Make brief notes on everything you can recall from that period, including physical details of places and things, other sensations, such as smells or tastes, feelings you experienced at that time, and so on. Variation: Meditate after selecting the period and before making notes. Variation, based on a suggestion by Eda LeShan: Without taking time to think or select, write down a series of memories that come to mind, up to ten of them. Try to identify a theme or feeling that ties these memories together.

Memory-Stretching Games and Pastimes

Several kinds of popular games and other activities exercise all three levels of memory, some drawing on recognition, some on recall. Enjoy yourself while you give your memory a workout with these:

Bridge (card game): Remembering bids and cards played is good practice for intermediate recall.

Scrabble and other word recall games: Long-term recall of words with specified letters. Variation: Create your own solitaire word games with a set of letters. For example, draw fifteen letters and try to use them all in words that can be found in the dictionary, and keep drawing letters until you make words with as many of your letters as possible. You don't necessarily have to form crosswords.

Crossword and acrostic puzzles: Long-term recall of words briefly defined, possibly with specified letters.

Concentration (traditional card game or TV game): Both short-term and intermediate-term recall of locations of cards or letters.

These suggestions may remind you of other games that may also give you memory practice.

GETTING PERSONAL

Try at least one of the memory exercises. Better yet, select and carry out an activity for each of the three levels of memory: short-term, intermediate-term, and long-term. Doing so will show you what level needs the most practice, and whether you want to work on recognition before you improve your recall.

Consider spending a few minutes every day for at least two weeks repeating the exercise or trying new ones.

After you have tried memory exercises for several days or weeks, take credit for any improvements you see or any satisfaction you feel. As with other forms of exercise, at least you'll feel better for doing something about your memory—for being interested enough to take planned steps to use it so you don't lose it.

9

Health and Diet: Keeping Well Naturally

Question to Mr. Cayce in trance: Is there the likelihood of bad health in March?

Answer: If you are looking for it, you can have it in February. If you want to skip March, skip it, you'll have it in June. If you want to skip June, don't have it at all this year!

EDGAR CAYCE reading no. 3564–1

THE SPIRITUAL SOURCE OF Cayce's information was not above gently chiding the questioner, trying to make a principle very clear. In the above reading, given in January, a woman in her forties asks for a prediction about possible illness in March. The reading tells her that she can be ill whenever she chooses to be, and she can also choose not to be ill at all!

Through your "conventional eyes," the condition of your physical body and the state of your physical health are perceived to be the result of the food you eat, the exercise you get, and the health precautions and safeguards you observe. Through your "new eyes," you can recognize in your health another great play by your universal triple-play team, "Spirit to Mind to Body." The physical results from what precedes it first in the spiritual and then in the mental. Your body and your physical health, as well as your other physical circumstances, are at their most favorable when you are exercising spiritual disciplines, such as ideals, meditation, prayer, and dream work, and when you are effectively managing your attitudes and emotions, and appropriately applying your skills and abilities.

Of course, eating, exercising, and caring for yourself affect your physical condition, but whatever you choose to do at the physical level will operate through the environment you have established at the spiritual and mental levels.

In this chapter I address the physical body itself—its longevity, its health, and the diet and care that sustain it. And in the two chapters that follow this one, I will look at other elements in your physical world: your living conditions, your financial circumstances, and your interactions with the world around you through activity and service.

IS A PHYSICAL DECLINE INEVITABLE?

The preceding two chapters should have left you with a feeling of encouragement about your maturing mental abilities and memory as you grow older. Despite myths and uninformed opinions around you, you should have the mental capability of doing just about anything you want to do, given the opportunities and the necessary physical capabilities.

One conventional view of physical well-being as you age is presented by Erik Erikson in *Vital Involvement in Old Age:*

> With aging, as the overall tonus of the body begins to sag and innumerable inner parts call attention to themselves through their malfunctions, the aging body is forced into a new sense of invalidness. Some problems may be fairly petty, like the almost inevitable appearance of wrinkles. Others are painful, debilitating, and shaming. Whatever the severity of these ailments, the elder is obliged to turn attention from more interesting aspects of life to the demanding requirements of the body. This can be frustrating and depressing.

The unfortunate implication of such statements is that there is nothing you can do to avoid or change those conditions, that you should expect them to occur. Countering that conclusion are the results of considerable recent research in programs such as the Gerontology Research Center in Baltimore referred to earlier, the University of Michigan's Institute of Gerontology, the University of Southern California's Andrus Gerontology Center, and Duke University's Study of Aging and Human Development. The September 1987 issue of the *AARP News Bulletin* reports on a conference called The Promise of Productive Aging in which research scientists showed that today's elder defies the stereotype of "accelerating decline" with age, but instead appears to be "getting smarter, healthier, and more productive." The article reports:

> Addressing the question of changes in physical performance with age, the scientists stressed that effects of disease, abuse, or disuse should not be confused with normal aging. Gradual physical decline begins early in life: reflexes slow, hearing and eyesight diminish, and stamina decreases. But much decline attributed to growing older really results from lifestyle choices that can be controlled.

Two such choices are smoking and alcohol abuse, both of which accelerate the rate of aging and impose a higher risk of disease. Physiological factors, such as muscle strength and the capacities to consume oxygen or to metabolize sugar, decline with age, but can all be reversed with systematic exercise. Through their "conventional eyes," these scientists attribute the better health of elders to "better medical care, improved diet, and increased emphasis on exercise."

Studies that look beyond the salutary effects of physical care reveal not only the physical effects of attitudes and emotions, for example, but also the physical impact of spiritual practices, such as meditation. For example, research reported by David Orme-Johnson in *Psychosomatic Medicine* followed the medical care statistics of participants in a health insurance group where Transcendental Meditation (TM) was a requirement for membership. The results suggest that, not only do those who meditate regularly use significantly less medical service than those who don't meditate, but that the positive effects of meditation on health increase according to the number of years spent meditating. A growing number of studies are being directed to the physical effects of both spiritual and mental beliefs and practices. The prestigious Baltimore study concludes that those with a positive attitude throughout life age more successfully than those who foster feelings of uselessness, loneliness, and depression as they grow older.

You have a choice in how you feel about aging and its effects, and that choice will help to determine your physical condition. In Christopher Hallowell's book *Growing Old, Staying Young*, after reviewing "what medicine and science are doing to make aging a natural part of a healthier and longer life," he says, "As inevitable as aging is, it is a continuing process, the outcome of which is far more susceptible to our control than we have ever before envisioned." The wry response of the Cayce reading at the beginning of the chapter emphasizes this control you have over your health.

LONGEVITY AND REJUVENATION

Several people came to Cayce for readings on such questions as

What will be the span of my life here, so that I may plan accordingly? (no. 338–5)

I would like to know very much how long I will live on this Earth plane. (no. 694–2)

May I expect to have a long life in this experience? (no. 1233–1)

What advice should [this person] have from her forces that will aid her to live long and happily? (no. 325–21)

The Cayce readings on longevity and rejuvenation present the principles that follow for your consideration.

You have control over the length of your life according to your intentions, your thoughts and attitudes, and your actions. You may expect to live longer

if you work diligently toward your ideals and purpose;
if you become more and more helpful to others;
if you use your abilities in constructive and creative ways;

Furthermore, even the potential for physical renewal is within the human body. Life itself is part of the Creative Force manifested in you through electrical or vibratory forces. Those forces are affected by what you assimilate: "What we think and what we eat—combined together—make what we *are*, physically and mentally" (no. 288–38).

Every atom, every corpuscle of the body is life. Each cell is a world of its own and undergoes complete physical change every seven years.

When they are in unison, the cells may build everything necessary to reconstruct the body. Every atom, every organ can reproduce itself or its likeness by assimilating the correct fuel.

By creating in every atom of your body the knowledge of the action of the Creative Force, of God, as related to spirit, mind, and body, all three may be renewed. Thus the great commandment—to love God (the Creative Force) with all your heart, soul, mind, and strength—means to reach for the infinite resources available, to honor the guidance and direction from those resources, and to dedicate yourself to growing toward your ultimate purpose—Oneness with God. You are renewed physically, as well as mentally and spiritually, through such a commitment. John Wesley, founder of the Methodist church, said in 1747, "The love of God . . . becomes the most powerful of all the means of health and long life." And close to your love of God must be your love of others—Jesus's second commandment—a prerequisite for longevity, according to Cayce.

Thus the decision to live a long life depends on your choices about your spiritual, mental, and physical selves. Any regimen you adopt must include all three selves.

You may mentally direct that your body create within it whatever replenishing forces are necessary to overcome any disturbance of the sensory functions of the body. In fact, all healing of any nature must arise within yourself. To release useless physical conditions, there must be a change of attitude at both the spiritual and mental levels, as would be expected from the law that says, From spirit to mind to body.

To many people such concepts are untenable, as remote as they seem to be from the hard scrutiny of science. Yet with increasing frequency you see statements such as these:

No matter what the physical mechanisms of aging are and no matter what you eat or how little you eat, successful aging depends as much on attitude as on physiology. . . . [Psychologists'] principal finding is that you can exert some mental control over health and thus indirectly over longevity. (Christopher Hallowell, *Growing Old, Staying Young*)

Recent research has demonstrated the brain's ability to maintain its circuits and to repair them if damaged. The brain has growth factors (proteins) that form part of a self-healing process induced after injury. [Carl Cotman, professor of neurology at the University of California, Irvine] compared the brain to a self-repairing computer able to reprogram itself constantly. In effect, Cotman says, healthy cells "take up the slack and sprout new connections." (*AARP News Bulletin*, September 1987)

Nerve cells [in the brain] can grow at any age in response to intellectual enrichment of all sorts: travel, crossword puzzles, anything that stimulates the brain with novelty and challenge. (Roger Walsh, medical school psychiatrist, University of California, Irvine, quoted by Daniel Goleman in Ft. Lauderdale *Sun-Sentinel*, August 20, 1985)

Walsh's comment provides physiological support for the suggestions in Chapter 7 for keeping up the learning and mental stimulation process throughout your lifetime.

THE HEALTH OF ELDERS

Medical and psychological experts agree that the physical and mental health of the elder are so intertwined that isolating and treating individual health problems is difficult. They further agree that many of the mental and physical problems develop from factors under the individual's control: excess weight, high cholesterol, alcohol abuse, tobacco use, stress, and, to some degree, environmental factors and high blood pressure.

The Cayce readings state repeatedly that good health and balance in the bodily systems are normal conditions, and that you are personally responsible for poor health and imbalances. The readings acknowledge the value of necessary medical treatment and medication, the key word being *necessary*. Excessive external treatments and medications may lead to dependency on them. Also, some treatments are for symptoms, not the internal causes, so the problems continue, perhaps in another form. The treatments may in themselves cause new problems, according to Cayce.

Two of your most critical responsibilities in maintaining your health are assimilations and eliminations. In one reading Cayce says:

> If the assimilations and eliminations be kept nearer *normal* in the human family, the days might be extended to whatever period as was so desired. (no. 311–4)

Assimilations include everything taken into the body, mentally as well as physically. A later segment of this chapter summarizes Cayce's views on diet—the physical side of assimilation. Your responsibilities for what you eat and what you take into your mind are clear enough.

The body has four elimination systems: the skin, the sweat glands, the lungs, and the alimentary canal, with separate processing of liquid and solid wastes. A primary purpose for the emphasis on bodily cleansing is to keep the skin clean and pores open for proper elimination through those systems.

The frequent suggestion to get out into nature must partly be to refresh the lungs, assuming you can find a place to breathe fresh air. Although Cayce does not ask people to stop smoking, he recommends everything in moderation. With the knowledge we now have about not only the effects of smoking today's cigarettes, but also the impact on others of secondhand smoke, keeping the lungs clean precludes smoking.

Where Cayce diagnoses toxins and undischarged substances in the body, especially in the colon, he recommends periodic colonic irrigation—a kind of enema that goes high into the colon. He also urges people to drink eight glasses of water a day to aid in internal cleansing and elimination.

A third type of system that the Cayce readings charge you with keeping in good operation is your circulation, including the flow of blood and neural impulses throughout the body. The frequent recommendations for massages and spinal adjustments are often aimed at removing circulation blockages and generally improving circulation.

The Cayce approach to health care can best be illustrated by his suggestions for three ailments occurring frequently in the older adult: the common cold, indigestion, and constipation. I'll also address an issue of frequent concern, although not of high occurrence: Alzheimer's disease.

The Common Cold

In a special reading on the common cold (no. 902–1), Cayce says that the cold takes almost as many different forms as there are individuals who contract it. But regardless of its form, Cayce says it is a "germ that attacks the mucous membranes of nasal passages or throat," and "is both contagious and infectious," especially if you come in contact with someone "sneezing or suffering with cold."

Apparently two conditions must prevail before you get a cold: you must be in a susceptible state for a cold, and you must experience one or more triggering factors. Regarding susceptibility, the acid–alkaline balance in the body seems to be the key to prevention. Usually a cold is contracted only when the body is in an acid condition, although overalkalinity can occasionally lead to a cold. Therefore you can reduce your susceptibility by following Cayce's recommendations that you choose foods so that your diet is about 80 percent alkaline-producing foods and 20 percent acid-producing. (Specific foods to maintain such a balance are discussed later in the chapter.)

The acid–alkaline balance in your body—and therefore your susceptibility to colds—is affected by other conditions besides the food you eat. The body tends to become acid when its vital energies are depleted through loss of sleep, activity leading to extreme tiredness, a detrimental change in the temperature of the body or the environment, or severe emotional upset from anger, resentment, or anxiety. Such conditions not only sap energy, but may also release poisons from the glandular system into the lymphatic system, which in turn blocks the eliminating channels, again creating acidity. Also, overheated rooms reduce the oxygen available to the body, resulting in a weakening of the germ-destroying forces in the blood. And eating food without thoroughly chewing it and using liquids to wash it down results in greater acidity and therefore greater cold susceptibility. You can therefore reduce your susceptibility to colds if you eat mostly alkaline-producing foods (such as many fresh fruits and vegetables), get adequate rest and sleep, avoid getting overtired, avoid extreme temperatures and overheated rooms, control your emotional reactions, and chew your food thoroughly. Not a simple remedy!

If your body is susceptible to a cold because your system balance is acid, then a cold can be triggered by any condition that causes a change in circulation affecting body temperature balance; for example, wet feet, a draft, a sudden change in air temperature, or being exposed to another person at the contagious stage of a cold.

Although the predisposing and triggering conditions differ from one cold to another, and therefore the specific prevention and treatment regimen may differ, several common rules emerge from the readings:

Maintain a regular sleep and rest schedule from day to day. Most people should have seven and one-half to eight hours of sleep every night. When symptoms of a cold appear, get more sleep and rest.

Drink plenty of water, preferably eight glasses a day. Lots of water is especially important during a cold; occasionally add an alkalizer, such as a teaspoon of baking soda in a glass of water. This will serve the dual purpose of helping to alkalize the system and also cleanse the body.

Maintain a healthy diet, particularly in regard to the acid–alkaline balance. During a cold a liquid diet is best, with virtually no meat and little other solid food.

Vitamins of all kinds are helpful when the body has any imbalance or weakness, because they help build the vital energies of the body. You should not, however, become dependent on vitamin supplements. Use them for two or three weeks and then set them aside for a week so the body can remember how to extract the vitamins from the normal diet.

Recurring weaknesses or deficiencies in the system, such as constipation or strain from an injury, should be acknowledged and corrected through appropriate treatment. Anything in the body that depletes the vital energies or that blocks the critical processes of assimilation, elimination, or circulation is another factor that potentially predisposes the body to colds.

Cayce's advice on colds, as on other subjects, was wide-ranging, yet often succinct: "Instead of snuffing, *blow!* Instead of resentments, *love!*" (no. 288–44).

Indigestion

According to the Cayce readings, a digestive disturbance of the stomach or the upper part of the intestinal tract originates either from excessive acidity (like the predisposition to cold susceptibility) or from a malfunction in the middorsal region of the autonomic nervous system. This latter condition affects the functioning of the liver or upsets the normal activity in the stomach when digestion starts. When the liver, pancreas, or spleen does not function properly, the circulatory system builds up "used, refused energies" that slow down or stop the assimilation of food. The accumulation of this waste disturbs normal impulses to digestion, which become magnified in their effect, resulting in indigestion. The stomach refuses to digest food taken in and the irritation increases and is prolonged.

Overcoming chronic indigestion requires cleansing and neutralizing the stomach, balancing the nervous system and its impulses to the critical organs, stimulating elimination, and restoring normal assimilation:

> The stomach can be cleansed by drinking large quantities of pure water. To combat acidity, Cayce suggests to several people "elm water," prepared by putting a pinch of powdered elm in a cup of water with an ice cube and letting it steep three minutes before drinking it cool. He also suggests tea made with saffron, to coat the interior of the stomach, before eating. Saffron tea can be prepared by putting three teaspoons of yellow or American saffron in sixteen ounces of water and letting it steep for

thirty to forty-five minutes. A teaspoon of milk of magnesia may also be taken after every meal to help cleanse and quiet down the stomach.

Balancing the nervous system is best done through regular spinal manipulation, with particular attention to the middle dorsal areas.

Elimination may be stimulated through colonic irrigations or mild cathartics.

Finally, proper assimilation can be restored through a diet that tends more toward the alkaline-producing foods.

Constipation

Dr. William A. McGarey in the *Physician's Reference Notebook*, which integrates the Cayce information with modern medical knowledge, says,

> Constipation . . . probably causes greater disturbance of function and more symptoms of disease in the human being than any other one single condition. . . . The consequences of constipation are consistently underrated, possibly because they are not understood.

As with the common cold and indigestion, constipation most frequently originates with an acid condition in the body, brought about by any of the same causes as outlined for the cold. And stress, tension, arguments, anger, and other negative manifestations of the adrenal gland create acidity in the stomach and duodenum. Excess stomach acid leads to decreased lymphatic function and liver inactivity, followed by decreased enzyme production and a decrease in proper assimilation, resulting in a reduction of the forces available for producing normal eliminations.

Then foods that were once acceptable become poisons, and the system becomes overloaded with used forces and intestinal wastes that begin to be reabsorbed through the lower intestine. A kind of intestinal indigestion occurs, causing a packing of fecal material in the large bowel. As waste is reabsorbed into the bloodstream, the condition is reinforced, further accentuated.

Constipation that recurs requires attention and correction through intestinal cleansing and an alkaline-reacting diet. Cleansing may be carried out through colonics or enemas, eliminants and cathartics, olive oil taken by mouth, and cleansing diets. Olive oil can also be absorbed in a massage that follows the path of the stomach from the duodenum to the jejunum and ileum, across to the caecum, and up over the ascending, transverse, and descending colon. A proper diet must be adopted and maintained consistently for a long period of time to overcome this condition.

Viewing these three common ailments—the cold, indigestion, and constipation—through the Cayce readings reveals the remarkable complexity of your body and its reactions to your use and abuse, and also reveals the equally remarkable simplicity of causes and corrections. Stated briefly, you must maintain an alkaline balance in your body, avoiding the mental and physical circumstances and activities that cause extreme acidity. An alkaline-producing diet is fundamental to both maintaining and restoring your normal healthy state. The critical bodily functions to keep in smooth operation are your circulation, assimilation, and elimination. If you add the essential restorative function of rest and recreation, you can summarize the Cayce health regimen in the acronym CARE—Circulation, Assimilation, Rest and Recreation, and Elimination.

Alzheimer's Disease and Other Dread Diseases

I follow my discussion of common ailments with information about a much less common, but highly publicized disease of the older adult. Alzheimer's disease (AD) is characterized by memory loss, confusion, mood swings, personality deterioration, bizarre behavior, wandering, paranoia, depression, combativeness and violence, and incontinence. Because many of these symptoms occur in forms of senile dementia that are reversible, accurate diagnosis is critical. Unfortunately the only completely certain diagnosis today is by examination of brain tissue, usually by autopsy after the person has died. Medical technology, however, has recently developed positron emission tomography (PET), resulting in a nuclear-imaging machine capable of revealing the workings of the brain cells. In 1986 there were only twenty-five such machines in the United States, apparently because of their enormous cost. They clearly hold promise for future diagnostic accuracy for AD. In the meantime, research continues to look for a biological marker in the blood, the cerebrospinal fluid, or the skin that will distinguish AD from other diseases and thus facilitate its early diagnosis. Specialists working with AD in research and practice have recently become optimistic about not only accurate diagnostic techniques, but also effective treatment, alleviation of symptoms, and an eventual cure.

Too often well-meaning but misinformed people assume AD has taken over when memory lapses or atypical behaviors occur, either in themselves or in others. Loss of memory is probably caused most frequently by disuse, excessive medication, or depression resulting from loneliness or other attitudes or emotions. And some changes in behavior and habits come about from other changes—retirement, living alone, loss of spouse or close friends, and lack of purpose or sense of direction. Accepting an amateur diagnosis of AD, or even a more professional diagnosis based solely on symptoms, lays the foundation for creating the conditions of AD through the operation of the powerful principle that "the mind is the builder."

What are your statistical chances of acquiring AD? Those older than sixty-five appear to be the most vulnerable, but recent studies indicate that if you make it to eighty-five, your chances of getting Alzheimer's declines. It is estimated that from 5 percent to 15 percent of adults older than sixty-five have AD. If you add that possibility to the statistics for heart disease and cancer, you could make yourself depressed over the possibility of getting one of these dread diseases in your later years. But as you grow in spiritual awareness, you recognize that statistics are not the basis for planning your life.

Consider the dynamics of becoming seriously ill. Some people may subconsciously believe that it is the only way of receiving the close attention and nurturing of others, perhaps twenty-four-hour loving care. In their book *Getting Well Again*, Dr. O. Carl Simonton,

Stephanie Matthews-Simonton, and James Creighton discuss the secondary benefits of illness:

> Illness includes much pain and anguish, of course, but it also solves problems in people's lives. It serves as a "permission giver" by allowing people to engage in behavior they would not normally engage in if they were well. Think for a moment of some of the things that people get when they are sick: increased love and attention, time away from work, reduced responsibility, lessened demands, and so on. Because cancer patients are often people who have put everyone else's needs first, they have obviously had difficulty permitting themselves these freedoms without the illness.

For some, the possibility of death through a legitimate disease such as cancer or even AD may seem to be the way out of an otherwise meaningless life. Research by Simonton and Matthews-Simonton suggests that cancer may occur in people who find themselves caught in untenable circumstances from which they perceive no way out. If you consider the earlier discussion of the effect that spirit and mind have on the cells in the body, you will realize how cancerous cells could in fact be created by attitudes of despair and hopelessness.

The choice to become seriously ill, even to have cancer or AD, is probably never made at the conscious level, but conscious attitudes and emotions plus inner subconscious understandings about life and its purpose act together to bring about the choice. When the low point of despair is reached and the individual's subconscious considers the possibility of cancer or AD, the will can still choose health. Somehow you must school your total consciousness in such a way that alternatives such as these are never considered. If the choice is cancer, the process apparently takes from six months to a year from the critical moment of surrender to circumstances to the appearance of cancer. Because the Baltimore longevity study shows that the immune system becomes less able to kill tumor cells after the age of forty, it's not surprising that the incidence of cancer is higher for older people.

Simonton, Matthews-Simonton, and Creighton describe the mental steps by which a cancer patient can change the illness back to health. The key again is the individual's will: the patient chooses to alter behavior, to be a person who reacts differently to the situations that caused the cancer. The body responds to the feelings of hope and the renewed desire to live. The recovered patient is sometimes mentally healthier after recovery than before the cancer occurred.

There has long been information available about Type A and Type B personalities and their differing susceptibilities to heart attacks, for example. Drs. Meyer Friedman and Ray Rosenman define the Type A behavior pattern as including the following kinds of traits: The Type A person is impatient at the speed with which events take place, moves and eats rapidly, often thinks about or performs two or more things at once, evaluates activities in terms of numbers, feels guilty about relaxing and doing nothing, always tries to do more and more in less and less time.

In their book *Type A Behavior and Your Heart*, the two heart specialists provide guidelines for the Type A to change his or her way of life and personality, including a drill against "hurry sickness." And as to whether it is worthwhile to change personality in the later years to eliminate Type A behavior, they say, "We will never, never believe that it is ever too late to aid [a Type A] person by taking away one of the major causes of his [or her] disorder."

In other words, if I realize I am a Type A and what that predisposes me to, I can make a choice to alter my susceptibility. Here again, if I have an understanding of life's ultimate purpose and my responsibilities for making progress toward Oneness, I am more likely to "choose life," recapping the Deuteronomy injunction. And if I move from Type A behaviors toward Type B behaviors, I place myself among those with a lower probability for heart attack, according to the statistical tables.

One of my conversation partners is a woman in her mideighties who is severely disabled by arthritis. She has had repeated setbacks over the past fifteen years, in both her physical condition and in her family, and yet she continues to be as active as possible in her residential care community. Her personal paradigm has gradually changed as she has studied the spiritual philosophies of several new age writers and tried to come to grips with the issues of responsibility for her circumstances and learning from her stumbling blocks. The statement that follows is a condensed and paraphrased summary of her outlook today:

> I wish I had understood some of these ideas earlier, like when my son was killed in an accident years ago, and when my husband walked out on me. I might have been able to deal with those situations in such a way that I wouldn't be where I am now, so crippled up and confined. I'm still not sure about the lessons I am supposed to be learning from all this, but I know there is a purpose to this and for my life. I can certainly deal with life better now than ever before. I'm being put to the test now to understand the lesson of my grandson's addiction to drugs.

My friend handles her disability and all the limitations it imposes on her with considerable grace and good humor.

My conclusion about Alzheimer's and other dread diseases is that you must not see yourself as affected by statistical probabilities for contracting such diseases, because you can take an initiative that keeps you from choosing such illnesses, just as you can prevent other forms of unwellness by your choice of spiritual, mental, and physical actions. I'll summarize this view of health and healing before I go on to the subject of diet.

WHY YOU GET UNHEALTHY AND
HOW YOU GET HEALED

From the research reports I have read, from my experiences with those who have had cancer or AD, and from my study of the Edgar Cayce readings, I have arrived at this understanding about health and healing:

Health and wellness are your natural state. You become ill or disabled through your deliberate actions, subconsciously chosen in one of two patterns: either you adopt physical or mental habits that give you immediate and ongoing gratification, habits that over time bring imbalances that affect you physically; or your subconscious perceives that an extreme condition of disease or disablement will gratify you in a way you cannot achieve while healthy.

A personal health maintenance program therefore requires you to search for signs of either of these patterns, using not only your conscious mind, but also dreams and intuition.

If illness or injury occurs, healing can begin when you first acknowledge that you were responsible for your illness or injury, and healing continues as you develop your understanding of the patterns of its occurrence and the reasons for your choices. Healing makes its greatest strides when you change those choices and adopt habits that reestablish balance. Visualization and the directing of energy through healing prayer and therapies such as laying on of hands, therapeutic touch, Touch for Health, and Reiki healing are effective aids to healing if such techniques are consistent with the beliefs of the person being healed.

This is not a view that is easy for everyone to accept, and I recognize the heavy burden of responsibility it lays on the person who is ill or disabled. As with some of the other concepts in this book that you may have found difficult to accept, I suggest you suspend your judgment for a while, rather than discard the possibility. Go along with the following exercise in the name of keeping an open mind.

GETTING PERSONAL

Over the past few years, have you experienced any ill health, recurring ailment, or injury? Have you had any colds, indigestion, or constipation? If your answer to both of these questions is no, you enjoy and deserve your good health.

If your answer to either question is yes, review several such occasions in your mind, and consider the following questions for each of them: What was happening in your life at the time? How long was your recovery time? Do you remember any special time when you felt you were definitely getting well? Try to recall as many feelings about each instance as you can. Make notes in your notebook.

Select one of these instances of illness or injury, and write more about the event, exercising your long-term memory, recalling additional facts and feelings about the experience. Who else was involved? Was anyone else inconvenienced? Was anyone drawn closer to you—or alienated from you—during the experience? Were any long-term decisions affected? Were any problems solved or created? Try to explore as many aspects of the experience as you can in your notes.

After using this form of memory, sit quietly after attunement through meditation, ask for additional information and feelings, and allow whatever comes to flow through your mind. Recognize intuitive information that flashes in. Have your notebook ready for taking notes, but try not to let note-taking disrupt the flow.

Consider asking for information in dreams, promising to remember and write down the messages you get.

After you have collected information and perceptions through the outer and inner approaches outlined, then consider the principles of what makes you ill, as previously discussed. Try to get an insight into the situation you are analyzing. Make notes of any ideas that come to you, without evaluating them. You need not reach a conclusion. Simply beginning to search for insight on illness you experience may trigger other ideas about what you can do to avoid illness in your life. Don't become negative or disparaging about yourself or the situation. Hold the view that this is a learning experience of great value, and be thankful for any insights you gain.

If you do not achieve any understanding that seems valid, repeat this session again soon, on a different instance of illness or injury. Let your inner self know that you are serious about understanding and controlling your health.

————————————

SELF-HEALING

I have mentioned my own experience fracturing a wrist and then participating actively in its healing. Instead of a recommended seven weeks in a full cast and four more weeks in a thumb splint, the total time of confinement was five weeks, and would have been shorter if I could have removed the cast. I never had to wear the thumb splint. The orthopedist expressed considerable surprise at the speed of healing, "especially at your age," demonstrated in X rays. I'm not sure he believed that I had no pain at the site of the fracture. On my last visit he cautioned that I might experience some discomfort off and on for several months. I have had virtually none, other than what I experienced for a couple of weeks as I retrained and stretched muscles and ligaments made lazy by immobilization.

I realized immediately after the injury (untimely as it was, with houseguests set to stay for several weeks) that I had somehow brought it about, and I began to identify reasons. I also began daily healing prayer for myself and for others, and weekly received a laying on of hands. I visualized healing, seeing the fracture as it appeared on the initial X rays disappear, with energy flowing across the fracture line. During this healing process I allowed the injury to interfere as little as possible with normal routines (including typing and cooking), finding alternative ways of doing two-handed operations. I discouraged others from making sympathetic comments or excusing me from my share of work. Insofar as possible I was trying to reestablish the conditions of a completely healthy wrist. Healing took place because I understood the reasons for the injury and believed in the self-healing process.

A more dramatic example of self-healing is that of spontaneous remission, the situation where a person diagnosed as terminally ill goes into remission without treatment. Many medical specialists deny the existence of remission, explaining it away on the basis of faulty initial diagnosis. In the spring 1988 issue of *Noetic Sciences Review*, Brendan O'Regan reports on the documented evidence on spontaneous remission:

> In two years [of looking through reports on spontaneous remission as far back in time as we could find them], we have been able to assemble, in hard copy, almost 3,500 papers from over 830 medical journals in 20 different languages. So this phenomenon which supposedly doesn't exist certainly has a lot of people writing papers about it.

I don't know the reasons for individual instances of remission, but I can hypothesize about some people sensing—perhaps intuitively rather than logically—that they have more control over their situation than others realize. They become confident that they have the ability to stop the process. A lot of prayer takes place, maybe along with some hard analysis of their lives, and they discover how much they have to live for. They ask and they are answered.

The principle to remember from this discussion of how you become ill and how you heal is that you participate in your own health to a far greater extent than you probably ever imagined. You can participate in maintaining good health—your natural condition—and if you are not totally successful at that, you can expedite your healing and recovery by your spiritual and mental actions, as well as by your physical actions. Complete healing cannot be a passive experience. To the question, "When will I be perfectly well?" a Cayce reading responded, "When you do that which will get you well" (no. 1131–1).

THE DIET OF THE OLDER ADULT

As you grow older you should maintain a healthy weight for your body size. Extra weight on aging bones and joints can tax energy at a time when it is already declining naturally. The superfluous weight puts an extra load on the heart and increases the possibilities for injuries from strains or falls.

Even when your body weight remains the same as you age, a larger proportion of that weight is fat rather than muscle, and fat burns fewer calories than muscle during normal activity. Therefore you require fewer calories. If your level of physical activity drops considerably, you may need to reduce caloric intake even further.

On the other hand, you need all the required nutrients in your diet, so you cannot simply reduce your food intake, if you have been getting what you need and maintaining a sensible weight level. Cutting down is not only unsatisfying to the palate, but unsatisfying to the body if the cutback means you receive inadequate nutrients. In other words, you may need to change your food choices to reduce the calories while you maintain nutrition—another challenge for the elder.

In many of his readings related to health, Cayce recommends the basic food components and their proportions in the normal diet. Cayce emphasizes a diet that maintains the balances within the body necessary for proper assimilation and elimination to avoid predisposing conditions for illness. Although his recommendations parallel many of the standard rules for a healthy diet, he adds some principles and guidelines that go beyond most recognized nutritional plans. Because his recommended diet also tends to use foods lower in calories, the Cayce diet is a sensible one to consider for your later years.

GETTING PERSONAL

Table 6 is a self-inventory of the foods you eat, comparing what you eat to the Cayce diet. By completing and scoring the inventory, you can assess where you stand. The inventory does not address the total quantity of food you eat, but only the healthiness of the diet, as measured against the Cayce diet.

Score the self-inventory by adding up the numbers you have circled.

Find the total in one of the following ranges:

65–80: Your diet follows many of the principles of the Cayce diet.

50–64: Your diet follows some of the Cayce diet principles. Either you do not eat large quantities of the preferred foods, or you eat a considerable amount of some nonrecommended foods.

25–49: Your diet varies considerably from the Cayce diet principles. You eat a lot of the nonrecommended foods.

3–24: Your diet is almost the opposite of the Cayce diet. You eat little of the recommended foods and a lot of the nonrecommended foods.

An outline of the Cayce diet follows, so you can readily determine what principles you observe and where you could make changes to your diet so it is more consistent with the Cayce diet.

THE CAYCE BASIC DIET

A simple way to review the Cayce diet principles is to divide foods into four groups and then discuss how to make choices from these groups. This approach was developed by the professional staff of the A.R.E. Clinic in Phoenix, Arizona. They work with the Cayce health

Table 6
Self-Inventory: How's My Diet?

Part A.
For each item listed, circle the number that best represents how often it appears in your diet.

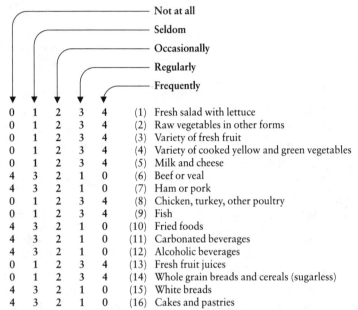

0	1	2	3	4	(1)	Fresh salad with lettuce
0	1	2	3	4	(2)	Raw vegetables in other forms
0	1	2	3	4	(3)	Variety of fresh fruit
0	1	2	3	4	(4)	Variety of cooked yellow and green vegetables
0	1	2	3	4	(5)	Milk and cheese
4	3	2	1	0	(6)	Beef or veal
4	3	2	1	0	(7)	Ham or pork
0	1	2	3	4	(8)	Chicken, turkey, other poultry
0	1	2	3	4	(9)	Fish
4	3	2	1	0	(10)	Fried foods
4	3	2	1	0	(11)	Carbonated beverages
4	3	2	1	0	(12)	Alcoholic beverages
0	1	2	3	4	(13)	Fresh fruit juices
0	1	2	3	4	(14)	Whole grain breads and cereals (sugarless)
4	3	2	1	0	(15)	White breads
4	3	2	1	0	(16)	Cakes and pastries

and diet principles in their therapies. Table 7 lists the four Cayce food groups and how they are to be incorporated into the diet. In more detail, the dietary principles are as follows:

1. For proper alkaline–acid balance, choose 80 percent of your daily food intake from food group 1, mostly fruits and vegetables. The other 20 percent should be largely from food group 2. Include foods from food group 3 about three times a week, and avoid foods in food group 4 altogether, except as noted.

2. Within food group 1, choose three aboveground vegetables to every root vegetable (potatoes, beets, carrots, and so on). Also choose one leafy vegetable to every pod vegetable (such as peas or beans).

Table 6, Self-Inventory: How's My Diet? (continued)

Part B.

For each of the following, circle the number in front of the choice that best describes how often the food appears in your diet.

A. Use of canned tomatoes and tomato products compared with fresh tomatoes:
   4. More canned tomatoes than fresh in my diet
   2. About the same amount of each in my diet
   0. More fresh tomatoes than canned in my diet

B. Proportion of root vegetables compared with vegetables grown aboveground:
   1. More roots than aboveground vegetables in my diet
   3. About the same of each kind in my diet
   4. More aboveground vegetables than roots in my diet

C. Proportion of leafy vegetables to pod vegetables (peas, beans, and so on):
   2. More pod vegetables than leafy vegetables in my diet
   2. More leafy vegetables than pod vegetables in my diet
   4. About the same of each kind in my diet

D. Combination of coffee with cream or milk, or combination of citrus (for example, orange juice or grapefruit juice) and milk or cereal at the same meal):
   0. I have both of these combinations regularly in my diet.
   2. I use one of these combinations regularly, but not the other one.
   4. I don't have either combination regularly in my diet.

3. Eat many of the vegetables raw, especially celery, lettuce, carrots, and onions. Use fresh tomatoes and cabbage in moderation.

4. Use potatoes sparingly in the diet, being sure to include the skin. Use plenty of peas, beans, and other pod vegetables, especially cooked from a dried form. Use more canned tomatoes and tomato products (paste, sauce, and so on) than fresh tomatoes.

5. Acid-producing foods include starches, fats, and sugars, many of the foods in food group 4.

6. Eat lighter meats, such as poultry and lamb, plus fish, more than heavier red meats, such as beef and pork. Avoid consuming the grease produced in cooking meats and fish. Beef marrow, beef juice, beef broth, and beef liver are exceptions to the limitation on beef; they have special body-building forces.

Table 7
The Cayce Diet Food Groups

Food Group 1 (About 80% of daily diet)	**Food Group 2** (About 20% of daily diet)
Fresh fruits of all kinds	Dairy products, including whole, skim, or powdered milk, yogurt, buttermilk, butter
Yellow and green vegetables grown aboveground, including leafy vegetables and pod vegetables, both cooked and raw	Poultry, lamb, and fish
Root vegetables, including potatoes, beets, carrots, onions, etc.	Whole grain cereal (no sugar added to product or at eating)
Fresh fruit and vegetable juices	Whole grain breads or wafers (without white flour or sugar)
Herbal teas	Honey
	Soups

Food Group 3 (About 3 times a week)	**Food Group 4** (Avoid these, except as noted)
Eggs	All fried foods, including potato and corn chips
Cheese	Candy
Potatoes with skin	Cakes and pastries
Whole grain rice	White bread and other products using white flour and white sugar
Foods prepared in gelatin	Pasta, including macaroni, spaghetti, and noodles
Ice cream, custards, puddings (in moderation)	Cereals with sugar coating or added sugar
Cooked fruits	Carbonated beverages
Mayonnaise and cold-pressed oils (sunflower, safflower, olive, sesame, etc.)	Alcoholic beverages (wine in moderation)
Nuts	Pork (except occasional crisp bacon)
Spices and condiments	Processed foods, such as TV dinners, etc.
Beef	

7. Avoid certain food combinations at the same meal:

   Don't eat citrus or other acid-forming fruit (such as apples) or tomato juice at a meal when you eat whole grain cereals. Whole grain bread is all right in combinations.

   Don't eat quantities of starches with meats or other proteins.

   Don't have orange juice and milk at the same meal.

   Don't add cream or milk to coffee or nonherbal tea.

8. For sweeteners, beet sugar and grape sugar are preferred. Honey can be used in moderation, as can saccharin and brown sugar.

9. Gelatin acts as a catalyst to increase the absorption of the vitamins in vegetables, and can be sprinkled on in dry, unflavored form, or used in gelatin salads. Avoid gelatins with added sugar.

10. Drink six to eight glasses of water a day, especially before and after meals. One routine to consume eight glasses of water a day: drink one glass before and after every meal, one on arising (preferably warm), and one before retiring. The water aids in both assimilation and elimination, especially the latter.

Most elements of the Cayce diet parallel many other basic diet and nutritional recommendations, with some notable exceptions, such as the food combinations and the balance among types of vegetables. In an AARP booklet by Dr. William J. Bicknell, titled *Strategies for Good Health*, a list of tips for a healthful diet is similar to the basic Cayce recommendations, with an added emphasis on using low-fat dairy products, reducing sodium, increasing calcium (especially for women), and adding bran for roughage (a boost for elimination).

In Edgar Cayce's words, vitamins are "the creative forces working with the body-energies for the renewing of the body" (no. 3511–1). The Cayce readings recommend getting most vitamins from the foods consumed, but indicate that vitamin supplements are acceptable substitutes. If supplements are taken, however, they should periodically be discontinued, so the body doesn't rely on them. One cycle suggested is two to three weeks on and one week off, and then repeat the cycle.

To conclude the discussion of food and diet, remember that the food recommendations are designed to maintain the proper alkaline–acid balance, facilitate assimilation and elimination, and keep the body-building and energy systems active.

EXERCISE AND SLEEP

According to the AARP booklet titled *Strategies for Good Health*, a regular program of exercise for elders can:

> help keep joints mobile and maintain muscle mass
> promote cardiovascular fitness
> aid in weight control
> contribute to better sleep
> promote a sense of self-confidence and well-being

The booklet recommends an aerobic activity that exercises the heart and lungs, such as swimming, walking, or biking—all fairly easy on bones and joints.

An excellent series of graded exercises in strength, flexibility, and endurance, designed by Dr. Richard O. Keelor, is available from AARP in a fitness book for seniors called *Pep Up Your Life*. The booklet, originally prepared by The Travelers Insurance Companies, reports that less than half of those older than sixty engage in regular, vigorous exercise, yet believe they get all the exercise they need, probably not knowing what good exercise really is.

In reviewing Cayce's suggestions on exercise, remember his focus on CARE—circulation, assimilation, rest and recreation, and elimination. His recommendations repeatedly relate exercise to improving circulation, sometimes to facilitating assimilation and elimination, and occasionally to getting enough rest and recreation.

The Cayce readings frequently mention moderate levels of exercise, often as a form of recreation or being in nature:

> Walking is the best exercise, but don't take this spasmodically. Have a regular time and do it, rain or shine! (no. 1968–9)

Cayce also recommends swimming. If you want to add a special spiritual quality to your walking or swimming, consider adding a rhythmic affirmation to your activity. One I use is, "My body, mind, and soul are one, and I am one with God." This has a two-syllable beat that can be adjusted to the pace of your stride or stroke: "My *body*, *mind*, and *soul* are *one*, and *I* am *one* with *God*."

Two other forms of regular exercise are recommended. One of them Cayce calls the cat exercise: picture a cat when it first wakes up—rise on your toes, stretch your arms overhead, and rock back and forth on your toes and heels. Fully stretch and get the circulation moving. If you're able, add bending to this stretch—bend at the waist from side to side and from front to back. Probably Cayce's most recommended exercise for circulation is the head and neck exercise, as discussed in preparing for meditation in Chapter 4—moving the head in all directions, forward and back, side to side, and then in circles in both directions. I personally find this helpful many times during the day, especially when I have been sitting for a long time.

As to sleeping habits, the readings emphasize the need for regular rest and sleep, most often suggesting seven and one-half to eight hours a night. (That will give you plenty of opportunity for experiencing dreams.) As an elder you may need even more rest. Rather than adding time to the night's sleep, rests or naps during the day allow renewal to occur when the energy drops off, so you avoid getting overly tired. If you meditate regularly, you may find you need less sleep, because meditation can both relax and energize the body.

Remember that the most physical part of you—your body—is so intertwined with the spiritual and mental parts that I have not been able to talk about health or diet without repeated references to the other parts. Answering a question about how to render the highest service in business, society, home, and with others, Cayce replies

> Keep self well-balanced, and keep the body physically fit, the mental body alert and the spiritual body—give it an opportunity to manifest!
> (no. 342–1)

10

Living Conditions and Financial Circumstances: When Enough Is Enough

Work where you are. . . . Begin where you are. If there are the needs for other environs, these . . . will be given thee.
EDGAR CAYCE reading no. 4021–1

Let the financial be the result of honest, sincere desire to be and to live so that others may know the way also. God giveth the increase.
EDGAR CAYCE reading no. 2409–1

W HEN I ASK A friend who seems to have all the time in the world to go with me to a concert or a movie or a meal out, I'm no longer surprised to hear, "I just don't have time today. I've got to mow the lawn." Or, "I have to stick around waiting for the furnace people to arrive." Or, "The kitchen faucet needs fixing." Sometimes the hesitation is followed by, "I'd better not. I've got to watch my pennies," with the suggestion of a rainy day to follow.

Although your living arrangements and your finances do influence how you spend your time, the first reading quoted points out that you can work wherever you are, and you may only be building frustration and resentment by wishing you were somewhere else with more resources at your disposal. It's easy to allow your physical circumstances and resources to control your activities to a greater degree than necessary. I'll put these factors into perspective.

LIVING ARRANGEMENTS IN LATER LIFE

Picture two women, Margaret and Helen, both in their seventies, with similar abilities and good health, both eager to live useful, meaningful lives in their later years. The living arrangements each has chosen greatly influences the kind of life she leads.

Margaret lives alone on the outskirts of town in a house she has owned and lived in for many years. Most people older than sixty-five live in their own houses or apartments, like Margaret does; almost 40 percent of women older than sixty-five live alone, in contrast to 15 percent of men older than sixty-five.

Helen also lives alone, but in a small apartment she rents in a senior community to which she moved only recently, partly because it was near a large shopping area in town. Only about 5 percent of those older than sixty-five live in age-segregated housing, like Helen does.

Margaret must drive, use a taxi, or ride with friends to run errands, shop, attend meetings and social events, or do volunteer work. Furthermore, she must spend some time every day preparing meals for herself and taking care of household needs. Occasionally she must arrange for repairs to her appliances or buy replacements for them as they wear out, and she has a small yard she takes care of herself or with assistance. The demands of her living circumstances consume a considerable amount of her energy, as well as her time. Maintaining a home continues to be a major focus of her life.

Helen is within walking distance of a large shopping area and is close to a bus line that is reliable. Her home chores are minimal, including her meal preparation, because she eats many of her noon and evening meals in a dining room in the retirement community or in nearby restaurants. She volunteers in a hospital, in the office of a social agency, and in her church. The focus of her life is outside her home.

Margaret has the security of owning her home debt-free; she has plenty of room for the attractive belongings she has acquired over the years; she has all the privacy she wants; and she has space to accommodate occasional out-of-town guests and to have social evenings with friends.

Helen is responsible for a monthly rent that will rise as years go by; she could even find herself having to move if it becomes too expensive or the community closes or her building is torn down; she had to give up most of her furnishings and possessions to fit herself into a two-room apartment; the walls seem thin and she has to be careful about the volume of her radio or television; she does little entertaining, and her out-of-town visitors must stay at a nearby motel.

As these two situations illustrate, whatever living arrangement you have will either limit or facilitate your way of life. Every alternative has its enhancing and its limiting considerations. As you decide how you want to use your time in your later years, you must consider the choice of way of life and living accommodation from those available. If you want your focus to be away from yourself and toward involvement with others, you may need to put yourself in situations less oriented to the home, regardless of what your previous circumstances have been. With years behind you of living a certain way, decisions to change your living arrangements can be challenging, even more so when you live with others.

Many decisions about where to live in the elder years are made in times of crisis—after the death of a spouse, or when physical incapacitation precludes driving a car or using stairs or caring for a home. Many people plan where they will live after retiring from full-time work in the early phase of the elder years—the fifties and sixties. Few seem to consider the possibility that the postretirement living arrangement may have to be reconsidered in the seventies or eighties or beyond.

Most people living in their own homes seem to want to stay there as long as possible, and it may be healthiest mentally and physically for them to do so if they can get the assistance they need for the everyday tasks of self-care and upkeep of the household. Such home help resources are not in plentiful supply in many parts of the United States (in contrast to the Scandinavian countries, for example), and their cost may exceed the ability of the elder to pay for them. At the very least, the elder should have up-to-date lists of critical services in the community, such as visiting homemakers, special transportation services, and meal delivery.

What guidance is in the Cayce material for this choice of where and how you live in your later years? Here are some considerations:

Make the most of wherever you are. Cayce frequently reminds you that you have put yourself where you are for a reason, and you should accept these circumstances as the best way at the moment to accomplish your ideal and purpose. If you keep those as your focus, you will find ways of moving toward them in spite of what seem to be limiting conditions: "Do not count any condition lost. Rather make each the stepping-stone to higher things, remembering that God does not allow us to be tempted beyond what we are able to bear and comprehend, if we will but make our wills one with His" (no. 900–44). This does not mean ignoring a need to change living arrangements when conditions warrant it.

Be sensitive to God's guidance. If you are considering a move, work with your dreams as well as with prayer and meditation to seek assistance. Watch for signs and intuitive information that trigger alternatives or clues about timing. To a fifty-six-year-old woman asking about a change in her life activities as well as a change in where she lives, Cayce responds, "Use with all thy might what thy hands find to do, where ye are; and when it is time to move, let Him guide thee where to go" (no. 2608–1). Also use the Cayce-recommended decision-making process, summarized succinctly in one reading:

> Ask self in [your] own conscious self, "Shall I do this or not?" The voice will answer within. Then meditate, ask the same, Yes or No. You may be very sure if thine own conscious self and the divine self [are] in accord, you are truly in that activity indicated, "My spirit beareth witness

with thy spirit." You can't get far wrong in following the word, as ye call the word of God. (no. 2072–14)

Other readings emphasize that the accord here includes the consistency of your decision with your spiritual ideal.

Arrange opportunities to help others.   According to the Cayce readings, helping others is one of the most important ways of growing spiritually toward God, regardless of age. This suggests giving priority in your choice of living arrangements to places where you will have opportunities to reach out to others, be of service to others, share your wisdom and talents with others—the focus of the next chapter.

Allow yourself to be helped by others.   Your needs may give someone else the opportunity to be of service. In your effort to maintain your independence, you may want to reject offers of rides to town or assistance with shopping or help with the lawn. Consider that you may be better able to keep the important part of your independence by letting others help you where they can, at the same time giving them a chance to be of service.

The main points about living circumstances are these: either adapt your living arrangements so they allow you time and energy to realize more of your life's purpose, or adopt new arrangements that will. Consider periodically the effect your circumstances are having on your life, and, when the balance is less than satisfactory to you, plan for a change. Don't wait until a crisis occurs that requires a precipitous decision that may cause you to settle for a lot less than if you had planned ahead. And perhaps most of all, act in accordance with your life's purpose wherever you live and whatever you have to do.

GETTING PERSONAL

Review your present physical living arrangements. Describe them briefly and list what responsibilities and tasks they require of you on a regular basis. Indicate where they give you freedom to pursue your ideal and purpose and where they seem to control you and limit your freedom. Write a note about your current mood or feelings about your living arrangements. Are you feeling especially good about them? Or is this a down period for you, and everything seems to be wrong? Try to get in touch with your feelings, and how temporary or permanent they are, concerning your present living setup. This note will be important when you reread your notes at a future time.

Next, develop one or more pictures of a changed situation that you believe would enhance your ability to accomplish your goals, including your spiritual commitments and your opportunities to serve. Include any ideas that occur on getting from the present situation to a better one. Take into account any changes already anticipated, such as a planned move to another home.

From time to time over the next several months, look back at these notes and add to them. Gradually develop a strategy for your future living circumstances that provides for a long-term arrangement with options for unexpected changes in your life. Be sure to take into account any swings in your mood or feelings about your present living situation. Remember that every arrangement has some advantages and some limitations, so don't let temporary discouragement propel you into a new arrangement. If you do this follow-up a few times over several months, you should be able to see the average of your perceptions.

FINANCES IN LATER LIFE

Many of today's elders experienced the Depression of the 1930s either directly themselves or indirectly through their parents. The result for some is an overdeveloped concern about financial security. And of course their minds are not eased by the knowledge that those sixty-five and older have the highest poverty rate of any adult group (more than 12 percent at the poverty level in 1986), with an income of $5255 or less a year for a single person, $6630 or less a year for a couple. Another 8 percent live at near-poverty levels—$6569 or $8287 annually, for single people or couples, respectively.

Some individuals seem to find comfort in their tight financial picture by saying that, according to the Bible, money is the root of all evil. The statement in 1 Timothy 6:10 is that the *love* of money is the root of all evil. In his readings Cayce says that some people have "earned the right of much of this world's goods" (no. 1901–1), sometimes through their actions in this life, sometimes through actions in a previous life.

On the other side of the issue is the question of how much money is enough. In research on the factors affecting satisfaction with life, psychologist Daniel Ogilvie of Rutgers University found that once a person had a minimum of money, life satisfaction depended mainly on how much time that person spent doing things he or she found meaningful. Finding that level of "enough" becomes significant, not just during your years of raising a family and your years of experiencing a job or a career, but even more so during your elder years, when your financial needs usually decrease. Near the close of *Passages*, Gail Sheehy says, "Would that there were an award for people who come to understand the concept of enough. Good enough. Successful enough. Thin enough. Rich enough." On the issue of material and financial security, the Cayce readings present the following principles:

You can obtain money and possessions beyond your needs when your life is guided by your spiritual ideal and purpose. How you then use what you have will determine whether you continue to experience material success in this lifetime or in subsequent lives. The goal must be to apply your resources while manifesting "the fruits of the spirit"—love, joy, peace, patience, kindness, goodness, faithfulness, gentleness, and self-control.

Stated another way, all you have is being loaned to you by God for the purpose of stewardship. Jesus's parable of the talents is an instruction on this principle (Matt. 25:14–30). If you use what you have in service to God, to the Universal Force, to realizing your ultimate Oneness with God, you will have what you need and even more.

The other side of the principle is that you should not seek material success and economic healing for your own selfish motives, self-indulgence, self-aggrandizement, or for "the abuse of the earth." If you violate this principle, your worldly goods may become "burdens to [your] conscience" and separate you from your home and your fellow human beings. Eventually your apparent success may fade away.

If poverty is not a virtue, if resources are available to everyone, and if you create your own circumstances through the spiritual–mental–physical sequence, why are so many older adults experiencing such great lacks? Your "new eyes" paradigm suggests several possible explanations:

Before coming into this life, they have chosen to work on the spiritual lessons of poverty.

Poverty in this lifetime is a karmic consequence of misused wealth and abundance in a previous lifetime.

Their motivations for money and possessions have been solely self-serving and materialistic.

Whatever resources they have had have not been used in ways that reflected the gifts of the spirit.

They have not been motivated to serve the needs of others, even with their nonmaterial talents and abilities.

Do such explanations allow you to write such people off? "After all," you may say, "they created their own situations. I have no responsibility or concern." True, they have brought about their circumstances, but the Cayce readings remind you that you are your brother's keeper. The poverty of others provides you with plentiful opportunities to serve them with your gifts, your time, your talents, and your accomplishments, as you would serve brothers and sisters in many other circumstances—not because you have in any way contributed to their condition and not because you want to manipulate their situation to your own advantage, but because they exist and have needs you can meet.

The Unity Movement, founded by Charles and Myrtle Fillmore, takes a strong and articulate position on your personal responsiblity for your prosperity. For example, in *Foundations of Unity* Frank Whitney says,

> God created you and placed in you a world of plenty. He has given you the mind through which you are given rich ideas. These ideas serve to relate you to abundance and success and to make them yours. If you do

not have prosperity, you may be sure that you need to increase your consciousness of prosperity.

Also in *Foundations of Unity*, Charles Fillmore himself is quoted as saying,

> The accumulation of riches . . . is futile unless it is the outgrowth of a rich consciousness. We advocate the accumulation rather of rich ideas, ideas that are useful, constructive, and of service to the well-being of all mankind. The outer manifestation of riches may follow or it may not, but the supply for every need will be forthcoming because the man of rich ideas has confidence in an all-providing power that never fails. He may not have an extra dollar, but his ideas have merit and he has confidence, a combination that cannot fail to attract the money to carry him forward. This is true riches, not an accumulation of money, but access to an inexhaustible resource that can be drawn on at any time to meet any righteous demand.

More recently, Arnold Patent has undertaken to help you understand and apply the universal laws through his writings, his workshops, and an ongoing network of people working with the laws in their everyday lives. His book *You Can Have It All: The Art of Winning the Money Game and Living a Life of Joy* is based on his belief, implemented in his own life, that you can have whatever you want and need in life if you work with the laws that govern the universe.

GETTING PERSONAL

Review your financial circumstances and how they affect your spiritual journey. Develop a picture of known and anticipated changes in your finances during your elder years. Evaluate the adequacy of the financial picture you paint for yourself. Consider how you have arrived at or will arrive at your financial circumstances, present or future. Have the Cayce principles been operating either consciously or subconsciously?

If you think it is needed, develop a picture of an enhanced financial situation with ideas on how to bring it about, following the preceding principles summarized from the Cayce readings.

The emphasis in the Cayce readings on service to others is not there solely to help you create or continue your prosperity. The next chapter, on the last of the building blocks, considers your responsibilities and needs for reaching out to others.

11

Involvement and Service: Reaching Out

Service . . . is the outlet through which the inner self may find the greater satisfaction.
EDGAR CAYCE reading no. 1046–1

As Sarah-Patton Boyle relates in her book *The Desert Blooms: A Personal Adventure in Growing Old Creatively*, she feels both liberated and abandoned as she approaches sixty. Her children have long since left home and recently her husband has walked away. Alone, she no longer needs her comfortable home of many years. Moving to a small apartment in a big city, her initial feelings of novelty and freedom gradually wane, leaving her immobilized. As she tries to connect with new acquaintances in her community and in her church, she discovers she is being treated as one of the "oldpeople," and feels as though she is "being elbowed out of the human race."

She finds little spiritual guidance even through her church, where she learns that the concept of a transcendent, personal God is passé, that secularism is fashionable. She finally accepts her despair and begins to live from day to day—a low point that becomes a turning point.

She reads about gerontology research and realizes she has no reason to avoid a more active life. She starts doing volunteer work with people older and less able than she is:

> I wanted to put my shoulder more effectively to other people's wheels. I had been taught that serving is our primary assignment. I knew from personal experience that helping others is the only way to truly belong to the human family. We are created as members of one body. When we fail to contribute to the welfare of another, we separate ourselves from the circulatory system, the nerve impulses, and the energy of the whole. When we opt for non-service, we condemn ourselves to internal isolation.

Even in that work she experiences some rejection and awakens to some new realizations about herself and her relationships to others through service:

> I felt wonderfully liberated when I ceased seeing a strong personal need to give as a dubious motive for giving [service]. There is nothing at all wrong with wanting to give—provided one does not let that need stand in the way of giving *only needed and desired* service to others. There is the rub. We often let our own need to serve overrule another's need for independence.

Many elders experience an emotional grab bag similar to Boyle's. Released from responsibilities that have consumed much of adult life—raising a family, maintaining a home, working at a job—they feel both liberated and abandoned. As they shift into a new way of life, sometimes in a new location, they encounter both kindly and not-so-kindly views about their capabilities, their usefulness, and their motivations. After satisfying long-held desires for the unoccupied time of leisure and relaxation, they discover within themselves a need that is now stripped of the obligations of family and finance—a need to help others. When they no longer *must serve*, they recognize the unvarnished *need to serve*—to be a functioning organ in the body of the human family, to extend Boyle's metaphor. And, like Boyle, they realize there is nothing wrong in wanting to give, as long as they give where it is desired.

Some people take advantage of their later years to volunteer regularly in organizations whose services they respect. Others prefer to serve in paid capacities when they can, particularly if finances need to be supplemented. Before considering specific opportunities for service, I'll look at Cayce's view of service as it relates to the elder years.

THE CAYCE VISION OF SERVICE

In my discussion of longevity in chapter 9, I said that the Cayce readings state that you can live longer if you work toward your ideal and purpose, become more helpful to others, and use your abilities in constructive and creative ways. Also, in my discussion of prosperity, in chapter 10, I said that you should use your talents and resources in service to God, manifesting the fruits of the spirit. To an older individual seeking guidance, Cayce says

> Learn, or teach, or train the body—not only to be good, but to be good *for* something. Let there be known there is a duty to self, and hope in service—for without service to the other, one may gain little in *this* experience . . . for Life itself *is* a service. Use, not abuse. (no. 53–1)

The implication here, made explicit in other readings, is that the development of your ongoing soul, your spiritual unfolding, progresses only through your successful experience in being of service to others.

What is there about service that gives you such a boost in spiritual development? The readings suggest at least three things. First, serving others provides opportunities to practice what you are learning about cooperation, love, patience, and other lessons along the path—opportunities you cannot receive any other way. The relationship you have with someone you are serving is unique in its impact on you. Boyle expresses it as "an inescapable partnership. We give by receiving as surely as by giving we receive." You do not expect a return on your service, but the value added is an experience of love.

A second way that service adds to your spiritual development is that it may help to raise the consciousness of others. Your acts of service may help others to perceive the effects of spiritual principles in action:

> Then the ideal is, "What may I do or be to others, that they . . . may have a greater concept of the purposes of life, by even being acquainted or associated with myself?" (no. 2030–1)

In being a model for others in your actions, however, you must avoid the traps of spiritual pride and self-righteousness—the pitfalls of "holier than thou."

A third way service furthers your spiritual unfoldment is its direct contact with God. Many readings include the statement, "Service to others is the highest service to God." You may begin to appreciate the immensity of that concept when you remember that you are created from the same energy force as God, and therefore you are a part of God:

> For in service to man is the highest service to the Maker, for man is that portion of the Maker which may be *physically* served. (no. 2901–1)

You are directly serving God when you serve the needs of another human being. In your inner life you acknowledge your reliance on God through prayers of, for example, praise, faith, and thankfulness. In your outer life you can give visible appreciation to God by giving your support to his physical presence in others through service—a remarkable realization.

Several cautions should be observed as you take advantage of service opportunities. The first concerns the "holier-than-thou" attitude just mentioned. One of Jesus' parables concerns a Pharisee who reminds God of his good works and his superior morality. Do you know individuals who like to remind you how much volunteer work they do, or how much their services are prized by those to whom they give them? Your reward for service is not in the recognition or praise, but in the doing. One reading says, "The *joy*, the peace, the happiness that may be ours is in *doing* for the *other* fellow" (no. 262–3). Ask yourself, Would I be doing this if absolutely no one knew about it and if I received absolutely nothing in return? In other words, is the service being performed unconditionally?

Boyle's recognition that the service must be needed and desired relates to the second caution about service from the readings: you are to "help others to help themselves," not to do for them what they can already do, "which makes them poor indeed" (no. 3575–2). It is often easier to do tasks for others instead of helping them do it. Consider helping a partially disabled person get dressed. It goes faster if you push the arms into the shirt and button it than if you hold the sleeves so the person can get into them, and help hold the shirt closed while the other person struggles with the buttons. Think of the patience both of you can experience!

A third caution is another chance to observe the principle of balance. You should never become so absorbed by the activities of service to others that you become one-sided, that you ignore your own needs in the pursuit of your ideal and your purpose. Cayce expresses himself pungently in a reading:

> For he that contributes only to his own welfare soon finds little to work for. He that contributes only to the welfare of others soon finds too much of others and has lost the appreciation of self, or of its ideals. (no. 3478–2)

GETTING PERSONAL

You have undoubtedly been of service to others many times in your life—probably to a greater extent than you realize. Think back over your life and find some of those times when you served others. Consider:

family	spouse
friends	children
relatives	coworkers
neighbors	members of groups
schoolmates	you belonged to

In your notebook list some of the events that allowed you to be of service to someone—especially the times when you gave that service unconditionally.

Your list should remind you of the feelings you had as you served, and encourage you to restimulate those feelings by once again reaching out to others in a spirit of service.

SERVICE AND INVOLVEMENT IN THE LATER YEARS

Isn't it time to sit back and let younger folks take over? After an active life of daily work and responsibilities for others, aren't I ready to disengage myself from the mainstream and drift into one of the quiet pools at the edge? Surely that's the way to find peace and satisfaction in my golden years.

The title of Erik Erikson's book presenting his research on late adulthood is *Vital Involvement in Old Age*. In it he says:

> We have selected a major theme for our presentation because it has proven especially illuminating and useful in our understanding of old age. As the title of our book indicates, this theme is *involvement*, and we have stressed the meaning of this word and its significance throughout life. That this involvement must be vital and include mutuality of experience is also one of our precepts; this is not surprising, since vitality is the very breath of the life force itself. . . .
>
> Elders, of course, know well their own strengths. They should keep all of these strengths in use and involved in whatever their environment offers or makes possible. And they should not underestimate the possibility of developing strengths that are still dormant. Taking part in needed and useful work is appropriate both for elders and for their relationship to the community.

In Christopher Hallowell's book *Growing Old, Staying Young*, he reports,

> The key to successful aging is involvement. People who age the best tend to be involved in various interests; they are involved with people; they are curious and they are flexible.

In *Our Best Years*, Helen Hayes cites psychologist Wendell Swenson's colorful statement on involvement:

> The human arena is where the action is. We would do better to stay in the center of it, displaying our physical as well as our psychological battle scars rather than covering them with an embroidered shawl. . . . We must remain on the "cutting edge" of life's experiences, with our peers *and* with younger people.

As an added comment on the last point, Erikson also stresses the need for intergenerational contact, involvement with people of different ages. He says, "To be constantly in the presence of those as old as oneself can be stultifying" (although many elders may not recognize this as deprivation). Today you hear about successful projects such as those where schoolchildren "adopt-a-grandparent" and regularly devote time to them; and those projects where residences for elders are located next to residences for children, with planned experiences for interaction.

Some values of such commitments are obvious: there is a greater motivation to keep yourself healthy and physically able, more interest in keeping up good habits of dress and personal grooming, and a need to keep your skills and abilities sharp and accessible, including your memories and your abilities to make decisions and solve problems.

As you continue to learn and grow through these experiences with others, you also become more reflective about yourself and about life. In *Passages*, Gail Sheehy points out that an increase in age is accompanied by a greater preoccupation with inner life, benefitting you "with two of the more salient characteristics of the mature years: insightfulness and philosophical concern." Furthermore, she says, as you age you come to approve of yourself regardless of other people's judgments. You finally achieve what Erik Erikson calls integrity, Sheehy continues, from which point you can "give a blessing" to your life. This interior viewing of yourself provides the needed balance to the act of reaching out to others, as suggested by the Cayce readings.

INVOLVEMENT THROUGH EMPLOYMENT

When someone seems skeptical about the employment of people older than sixty-five, you can point out that many of the largest companies are headed by elders, either as chief executive officers or as directors on their boards. President Reagan took office at the age of seventy; six of the nine current Supreme Court justices are older than sixty-five, four of them eighty or older; and the Senate and House of Representatives have many truly elder statespersons. One of the most outspoken advocates for the older American is Representative Claude Pepper of Florida, who was eighty-six when President Reagan, at seventy-five, signed into law the anti-mandatory-retirement bill initiated by Pepper. Thanking his colleagues for supporting the bill, Pepper said, as quoted in *The Virginian-Pilot*, October 27, 1986:

> If I had stopped serving in the public service, I do not think I would have been living for the last several years. It is good to have something to get up for in the morning, something to do, some challenge, that gives you somehow the impetus to carry on in spite of one's increasing years.

You're probably not considering employment in positions like these, even though some of those organizations would benefit by having a few more individuals motivated to serve and to be involved with life. (After all, Representative Pepper was first elected to the House when he was sixty-two!) You may want to consider part-time employment or self-employment, especially if you have been working full-time for someone else or if you are seeking employment outside the home for the first time. An increasing number of people are retiring in their fifties from their long-term employment, then reentering the labor market in jobs that are less demanding, less time-consuming, and even more satisfying than their career jobs.

Employers enjoy the many advantages of hiring older employees: experience in dealing with people, dependability, mature judgment, interest in part-time work, lower accident rate, attrition and sick time the same as for young employees, and a variety of available skills from past jobs or training. Recognizing the pluses of this "new" labor pool, several types of businesses have begun to recruit elders for jobs as office temporaries, fast food service workers, and bank tellers, to name those that have been publicized.

Today the employee eligible for Social Security pays a penalty for working in the years from sixty-two through sixty-nine). Currently, if your earnings from a job or self-employment exceed a limit ($6120 annually for those younger than sixty-five, $8400 annually for those sixty-five through sixty-nine), your Social Security benefits are reduced $1 for every $2 earned. Starting in 1990 that reduction will be less: $1 for every $3 earned. This disincentive no longer applies at age seventy, so those elders can work without such a penalty.

Self-employment is attractive to many older Americans, and, according to the December 13, 1987, article by Ellen Brandt in *Parade*, many of them are highly successful. Some people start businesses that are direct outgrowths of their long-term employment: a newspaper reporter-editor starts her own small publishing company, a telephone company manager becomes a communications consultant, an interior designer forms a company that installs high-tech domed kitchen ceilings. Others create businesses out of what had been hobbies or special interests: an airline pilot with a long-time interest in antiques explores museums and antique dealers in his destination cities and then retires to establish his own antique store; a fashion model trained many years before as an artist and designer forms a company to market handcrafted picture frames, desk diaries, and wedding and photo albums; and a long-time hobby writer (this is me) makes the transition from full-time to part-time employment and finally becomes a self-employed published writer.

There are probably more opportunities for employment at your age in your community than you imagine. If this is the avenue by which you desire to reach out to others in service, watch the help wanted ads, ask employment agencies and temporary service agencies, observe businesses where you see older employees and follow up with inquiries. When you approach a time of choosing where to apply or what job to accept, take time for meditation and prayer so that you choose your opportunities in accordance with your life's ideal and purpose.

INVOLVEMENT THROUGH VOLUNTEER WORK

If you decide to reach out by donating your time and service to others, you have a "volunteer's market." Many organizations could not function without volunteers. Here are some types of agencies and organizations that use older volunteers, as listed in the AARP booklet *To Serve, Not To Be Served: A Guide for Older Volunteers*:

> Schools, hospitals, community centers, senior centers, nursing homes, libraries, museums, zoos, animal shelters, parks, and recreation departments.
>
> "Hotline" phone centers, courts, special literacy programs, voter registration, places of worship, theatre groups, fire departments, police departments, social service agencies, and mental health clinics.

Maggi Kuhn has been one of the most outspoken leaders of older Americans ever since she organized the Gray Panthers in 1972 to liberate older people from "paternalism and oppression with which society keeps us powerless." In Dieter Hessel's *Maggie Kuhn on Aging: A Dialogue*, Kuhn suggests several unique roles that elders can take on, some of which would lead to volunteer activity in relevant organizations:

> Watchdogs of public bodies, guardians of the public interest and the common good
> Advocates of consumer rights and whistleblowers on fraud, corruption, and poor services
> Monitors of corporate power and responsibility
> Builders of new coalitions, such as the old and the handicapped
> Testers of new ways of life, such as small groups of activists caring for one another

Many localities coordinate the recruitment and selection of volunteers through a clearinghouse or voluntary action center. So the way to begin your search, if you have no organization in mind, is to check with such an agency, if it exists in your community. If not, you can call individual agencies, and you can watch the local newspapers, where many organizations seeking volunteers post notices of their needs.

Before you look at the opportunities available, review your goals for volunteering, focusing especially on your ideals and purpose. With those in mind, consider factors such as these, adapted from the AARP booklet *To Serve, Not To Be Served*:

How much time do I have to spend on volunteer work? What degree of ongoing commitment can I make—for example, a half-day every week, one hour every day, day or evening hours, and so on?

Do I want to work near home or can I travel some distance? How will I get there in all kinds of weather?

Do I want to work mostly by myself or around others? (Remember the desirability of contact with a range of ages.)

Do I want to work directly with clients, students, or others my age, or would I rather work behind the scenes, helping with the nitty-gritty that supports the direct service?

What kinds of services do I wholeheartedly believe in? What do I want to give my time for?

Where do I think my talents and experience will best fit in?

If you take on regular volunteer activities, you will help to reinforce the image of elders as a valuable resource if you stick to your commitment of time and conscientious service. When occasions require you to miss a scheduled volunteer time or event, the volunteer coordinators or supervisors will appreciate your letting them know you will be absent. Not getting a wage for services does not relieve the volunteer of the responsibility for dependability, and clear communication.

OTHER EXPRESSIONS OF SERVICE

In Soviet Georgia, where many Russians not only live long lives but are active throughout most of those later years, American visitors look for factors in the way of life to help account for the longevity. Two themes woven into their lives are generational continuity and involvement: the elders are integral members of a multigenerational family, sometimes living under the same roof with their children and grandchildren, more often in homes near them. They are truly respected for their experience, wisdom, and age. They live to watch the generations that follow them reach maturity and satisfaction, and in fact they help them with their responsibilities. In a 1988 PBS television program featuring filmed interviews with some of these elders, one of the Russian women in her seventies says, "The job of old people is to bring joy to our families. This, I think, prolongs our lives."

Commenting on the program, Maggie Kuhn concluded that the longevity was apparently related to the family mutual support system. She went on to say that some of the same effects could be achieved through "families of choice"—the members of which are not necessarily blood relatives. The life-lengthening effects are not dependent on kinship, Kuhn said, but on relationship.

You may be of greatest service to another within your own family, or, to follow Kuhn's idea, within a "family of choice." Those who find themselves as caregivers to an elderly disabled parent or friend, or to a handicapped relative or neighbor, may serve best those who are closest. And many a grandmother is helping to tend the grandchildren and their home in these days of working mothers.

Accepting such responsibilities should not be without due consideration of ideals and purpose, sacrifice as well as satisfaction. An article I wrote for the September/October 1987 issue of *Venture Inward* entitled "Eldercare: A Challenge in Service" outlines the considerations and steps involved in such a decision, as well as some principles for elder care drawn from the Edgar Cayce readings. The suggestions include carrying out your responsibilities in a manner reflecting "fruits of the spirit" such as lovingkindness, gentleness, and patience; keeping outside influences constructive and creative; stimulating and stretching the elder with new and interesting experiences; and encouraging the study of chapters 14 through 17 of the gospel of John.

Beyond the immediate family are friends, neighbors, and others in your community who may need your help when it is offered with love and understanding. You could

Allow the neighbor's latchkey children to come to your home after school when their own home is empty.

Help to cook or take care of a yard for a friend during a period of
disability or illness.

Visit with residents of nursing homes who seldom or never receive visitors.

Allow guests of overcrowded friends to stay in your home while
visiting.

Write letters of support and encouragement to community
leaders.

Write letters of inspiration and uplift to friends and acquaintances facing special challenges.

Beyond your families and friends and the organizations needing
volunteers, there are uncountable opportunities for service when you
really look for them. Some will draw you together with others to
chart new ground, others can be done on your own. The following
list of opportunities is adapted from Harmon Bro's ideas for building
a new world in his article in the July/August 1986 issue of *Venture
Inward*. The ideas are culled from his experience in working closely
with Edgar Cayce.

Assist in starting and developing a self-help project—for example, a food cooperative, a hospice for the dying, a senior center.

Support a community of people who are working together to
build a better world—models include Findhorn, an Israeli kib-
butz, a Rudolf Steiner school, a Koinonia farm, and the A.R.E.
Clinic. Learn about the community, support its programs and
projects, offer volunteer assistance, pray for it, contribute to it
with money or materials.

Spend time cooperating with the Earth—find ways to save resources, clean up the environment, help others enjoy being in
nature, help in the protection of plant and animal life.

Help to sponsor one young person's education—not a family
member, but, in Bro's words, "someone chosen just for the adventure and the privilege." Help that person experience new
ideas, events, activities. Support him or her with prayers and

tuition assistance, if possible. Cayce himself did this with medical missionaries he recruited.

Finally, you may serve others best by demonstrating in your own life your experience with the universal principles guiding your life—the wisdom and vitality you have acquired by applying the spiritual, mental, and physical building blocks in your day-to-day activity. Whether you travel coast to coast in your recreational vehicle, meeting hundreds of people along the way, or stay close to home playing duplicate bridge, square dancing, or swimming in the Senior Olympics, you will have innumerable opportunities to be of service through the evidence of God in action in your life. In the winter 1987 issue of *Noetic Sciences Review*, Albert Schweitzer is quoted:

> I don't know what your destiny will be, but one thing I know: the only ones among you who will be truly happy are those who will have sought and found how to serve.

PART III

Promises to Keep

Promises to Keep

The ability to choose is will; as well as the ability to allow self to be used by influences.
EDGAR CAYCE reading no. 1608–1

You AND I HAVE come a long way together in this book. I began by asking you to examine your personal paradigm of reality—the way you look at life, at the world around you, and at the process of aging. I offered a view through "new eyes"—a view that incorporates some concepts and principles unfamiliar to many who have grown up in a Western culture. Then I presented a series of nine building blocks—spiritual, mental, and physical strategies with which you can build the future of your fifties, sixties, seventies, and beyond. Building with these blocks constitutes development in your spiritual nature, progress toward your eventual Oneness with God, growth in wisdom in its most fundamental form.

Whether or not you pick up these blocks and incorporate them into your life is a matter of choice. The distinguishing gift of your human existence is your will, so you can choose to grow now or you can choose to postpone your growing. And even if you do not consciously decide about your course of action, you have made a choice.

I presented the building blocks with recommendations for personal application. These exercises acquainted you with the concepts and techniques derived from the readings of Edgar Cayce. For these ideas and actions to have staying power, you must assimilate them into your life, integrate them into your daily thoughts and habits. I realize that the readers of this book differ in age, living circumstances, interest in new age thought, personal strengths and capabilities, and motivation to change. In part III you have an opportunity to plan your own strategy, level of commitment, and timetable, within a framework of balanced living in the elder years.

Chapter 12 shows you a menu of alternative approaches for implementing the building blocks in your own life. Chapter 13 presents the Cayce perspective of the well-balanced life, by which you can judge the quality of your life and the progress you are making in your spiritual journey.

You have a choice about how to spend the rest of your life. Choose to grow!

12

Choosing Your Path to Spiritual Growth

The soul grows upon that [which] it is fed. The soul of man is the greatest . . . of all creation, for it may be one with the Father. Little by little, line upon line, here a little, there a little—these are the manners of growth, that this [soul] may be one with Him.
EDGAR CAYCE reading no. 262–24

THE SPIRITUAL PATH IS like any other road: once you know your destination and the means by which you can travel, you must decide on the schedule and the specific itinerary to get there. The nine building blocks in chapters 3 through 11 provide components of your transport that you can assemble in many different ways. Whatever you create should fit your style of living and your level of motivation reasonably well, or you won't stick with it long enough to get anywhere.

I hypothesize four motivation/style profiles for spiritual growth. With which of these do you identify most closely?

Table 8
Sample One-Month Growth Plan for the Totally Committed

BUILDING BLOCK	ACTIVITY	FREQUENCY
SPIRITUAL	Review original life ideals and purpose. Refine according to newer insights and understanding.	Once
	Develop new affirmations for ideals and purpose.	Once
	Meditate with 10 minutes of silence, with prayers at beginning and end.	Daily
	Program yourself to recall and record dreams.	Nightly
MENTAL	Select a quality or attitude in yourself you would like to change, or a relationship to improve. Develop two exercises on it.	Once
	Carry out your exercises as opportunities arise.	Daily
	Choose an interesting topic to learn more about during the month.	Once
	Read and make notes about your topic.	3/week
	Select a craft, sport, or physical activity to learn or improve your skill in.	Once
	Involve yourself in the selected activity.	2/week
	Work a puzzle or game that exercises your mind.	2/week
	Select a level of memory to work on (short-, intermediate-, or long-term). Create an exercise.	Once
	Practice your memory exercise at least 10 minutes.	Daily

Table 8
Sample One-Month Growth Plan for the Totally Committed
(continued)

BUILDING BLOCK	ACTIVITY	FREQUENCY
PHYSICAL	Select two food, diet, or health habits to change or improve upon.	Once
	Practice those changes.	Daily
	Develop an affirmation about your finances.	Once
	Use the affirmation whenever a financial concern or question of spending arises.	Daily
	Select and commit yourself to a service for the month, to an individual, group, or organization.	Once
	Perform that service faithfully as committed.	Regularly
ALL	Develop your growth plan for the next month.	Once

Totally committed: "I want to work steadily on the full range of building blocks for my spiritual development, and I will give it very high commitment and priority in my life."

Gently committed: "I want to work steadily on my spiritual development, but I want to do it at a gentle pace."

Experimentalist: "I want to try out some of the ideas in a researchlike way, and find out for myself what works best in my life."

Topicalist: "I want to work with some topics extensively, and may never work with others."

You can be committed to a range of activities and still add an experimental or a topical emphasis to your plan, so you may want to combine one of the committed approaches with one or both of the other two.

Whatever profile you choose to follow, your chances for successful growth in that mode will be greater if you have a growth plan—

an outline of the activities you will try to carry out on a regular basis. As a start, I recommend planning one month at a time. This allows you to find out whether you have over- or undercommitted yourself and to make adjustments accordingly the next month. Or you might want to change topics or exercises, adjust to a change in your circumstances, or change from one profile to another. The monthly plan strikes a balance between committing yourself to meet an objective and letting yourself be flexible and accommodate to change.

Many of the activities within your growth plan will be exercises that you will define for yourself. Many people working with the Cayce materials refer to the disciplines they follow or the experiments they carry out. The exercise is to be an activity that will provide you frequent practice in applying the concept or principle on which you are working. For example, if you are working on overcoming a tendency to be critical or judgmental, one exercise might be to choose one hour every day in which you refrain either mentally or verbally from any kind of criticism of other people or circumstances. Remember, "little by little" is the theme of an exercise. You are not likely to change long-standing attitudes overnight, and so refraining from all criticism all the time would be unreasonable as a starting exercise.

Other exercises have been used throughout this book in the "Getting Personal" sections, and many of them can be incorporated into your own growth plans as you select related topics.

After you have completed several month-long plans, you may decide to switch to a three-month plan, perhaps timed with the seasons of the year. You can also gear the activities to the approaching season in its physical characteristics as well as to what it symbolizes. For example, spring is a period of new growth in nature and a time when you may be able to spend more time outside. So you can choose the themes of your growth plan accordingly—some elements may be new growth areas for you, and some of the activities in your plan may take you outdoors.

To get you started, I have outlined one growth plan for each of the four motivation/style profiles in tables 8, 9, 10, and 11. Regard-

Table 9
Sample One-Month Growth Plan for the Gently Committed

BUILDING BLOCK	ACTIVITY	FREQUENCY
SPIRITUAL	Review original life ideals and purpose. Refine according to newer insights and understanding.	Once
	Meditate with 10 minutes of silence, with prayers at beginning and end.	Daily
	Program yourself to recall and record dreams.	Nightly
MENTAL	Select a quality or attitude in yourself you would like to change, or a relationship to improve. Develop an exercise on it.	Once
	Carry out your exercise as opportunities arise.	Daily
	Choose an interesting topic to learn more about during the month.	Once
	Read and make notes about your topic.	3/week
PHYSICAL	Select one food, diet, or health habit to change or improve upon.	Once
	Practice the change.	Daily
	Select and commit yourself to perform a service to another person several times during the month.	Once
	Perform that service faithfully as committed.	Regularly
ALL	Develop your growth plan for the next month.	Once

less of which option you choose, I suggest you scan the outlines for all profiles. You may see ideas you want to incorporate into your plan. And you may wish to develop your own plan completely from scratch. Some suggested directions follow.

As you complete your plan or start to carry it out, don't look for specific results to occur or expect experiences or feelings to reflect

Table 10
Sample One-Month Growth Plan for the Experimentalist

BUILDING BLOCK	ACTIVITY	FREQUENCY
SPIRITUAL	Develop a schedule for the month to try out different preparatory steps to meditation, including experimenting with different aids to attunement (music, incense, chants, and so on).	Once
	Meditate following your experimental schedule. Keep a record of any experiences you have or any differences you detect in the quality of meditation. Try to relate them to the preparations.	Daily
	Describe several different routines for preparing yourself to recall and record dreams. Develop a schedule for the month to try out these different approaches.	Once
	Prepare for and record your dreams according to your experimental schedule. Keep a record of any differences that may be attributable to the method of preparation and self-instruction.	Daily
MENTAL	Create for yourself a test of your memory at all three levels (long-, intermediate-, and short-term). Test yourself.	Once
	Develop exercises for all three levels of memory, for use several times a week. Develop an experimental plan for practicing with the exercises in a pattern that may show some methods better than others.	Once
	Carry out your experimental practice plan.	Regularly
	Use the same or similar test to check results.	Once

Table 10
Sample One-Month Growth Plan for the Experimentalist
(continued)

BUILDING BLOCK	ACTIVITY	FREQUENCY
PHYSICAL	Describe in detail your day-to-day health, including sleep pattern; digestion and assimilation; frequency and types of headache, bodily pain, or other discomfort; elimination; symptoms of poor circulation; weight control.	Once
	Select one major change to make in your diet for the month, following the Cayce suggestions.	Once
	Make the change, and observe and record any reactions or differences in your day-to-day health or feelings.	Daily
ALL	Develop your growth plan for the next month.	Once

your efforts in predetermined ways. Accept that whatever you try is to the good, even if you are not aware of it. You are making your life more meaningful as you grow toward God.

GETTING PERSONAL

This is your last application opportunity in this book, and, in a sense, it is your final exam on growing in wisdom. Your objective here is to develop on paper your plan for personal growth during the next month, trying to establish a pattern that will continue month after month with refinements and changes in focus. You may adopt one of the growth plans in tables 8 through 11 and make it your own with specifics, or you may develop one uniquely yours.

Every plan should include activities from spiritual, mental, and physical building blocks, keeping a view toward balance. This balance is built into tables 8 through 11. You may find it helpful to

Table 11
Sample One-Month Growth Plan for the Topicalist

BUILDING BLOCK	ACTIVITY	FREQUENCY
SPIRITUAL	Identify a topic or technique from the spiritual building blocks (ideals, purpose, meditation, prayer, dreams) to concentrate on during the month. Develop a schedule of activities around that topic that involve you in a spiritual exercise daily. For example, the topic of ideals suggests a careful review and refinement of all your ideals, followed by daily exercises in which you focus on specific ideals. Your plan might include reading other material on the selected subject.	Once
	Carry out your planned exercises.	Daily
MENTAL	Identify a topic or technique from the mental building blocks (attitudes and emotions, skill or knowledge learning and practice, memory) to concentrate on during the month. Develop a schedule of activities around that topic that involve you in a mental exercise daily.	Once
	Carry out your planned exercises.	Daily
PHYSICAL	Identify a topic or technique from the physical building blocks (health and diet, longevity and rejuvenation, exercise, finances, living circumstances, service) to concentrate on during the month. Develop a schedule of activities around that topic that involve you in a physical building block exercise daily.	Once
	Carry out your planned exercises	Daily
ALL	Develop your growth plan for the next month.	Once

review the statements of mental and physical ideals you developed in chapter 3. Many of them can be converted directly into exercises in your growth plan.

Be as specific about activities and exercises as you can: for example, when you will increase your meditation from five minutes to ten minutes; which individuals you will concentrate on in working on your attitudes and emotions; what diet changes you will make and when.

Remember the little by little philosophy expressed earlier; don't try to change too much too quickly. It is better to start modestly and give yourself a chance to do more than you had planned, rather than to start out too intensely and have to do less than you had planned.

If you are in a close relationship with someone who is also interested in these ideas, consider developing joint plans or coordinated plans, so that you can share your experiences and your feelings as you proceed. Mutual reinforcement will go a long way in keeping you on target with your plan.

A final suggestion: as you work on your plan, use the guidance available to you through meditation, prayer, and dreams.

————————————

Enjoy your growth planning. Give yourself a special gift or privilege when you finish your plan and begin to carry it out. You are taking the initiative in shaping your own future, in controlling your own circumstances, in bringing yourself closer to Oneness with God. A celebration is in order!

13

Keeping Your Balance

Keep self well-balanced, and keep the body physically fit, the mental body alert, and the spiritual body—give it an opportunity to manifest!
EDGAR CAYCE reading no. 342–1

BALANCE IS A RECURRING theme in the Cayce readings. Some readings give a gentle reminder to maintain balance in dealing with specific situations; others exhort the listener to bring life more into balance or pay a penalty in physical or mental consequences; still others simply provide instruction on fundamental concepts and principles of balance.

Probably the most frequent references to balance relate to the individual's attention to balance among the spiritual, mental, and physical aspects of being. This undergirds all other types of balance, which is the rationale for planning your growth plans in chapter 12 to include activities in all three areas.

Balance does not mean equal attention or time to each aspect. Rather, you must find for yourself the amount of effort required in each factor to keep you moving forward on your journey, never ignoring any of them. According to the readings, it would be as inappropriate to spend most of your time on your spiritual disciplines as it would be to spend a majority of your time in either mental or physical pursuits. You are in this world to experience materiality and to use your will to deal with it in ways that will bring you closer to God. You cannot do that if you hide yourself from the world of the physical.

Reference to another kind of balance appears particularly in the readings for certain individuals: the balance between your work and your rest and relaxation. To one person Cayce says, "All work and no play is as bad as all play and no work" (no. 2597–2). And to another, "rest, play, work and think. Keep self attuned to consciousness of life in its entirety" (no. 137–125). The readings suggest that not only is relaxation essential for physical and mental well-being, but that it releases creativity and imagination and ultimately allows you to be more effective in and more satisfied with your work—a principle devout workaholics do not readily accept.

The Cayce material on diet and health is replete with principles of balance: balance between alkalinity and acidity in the body in a four-to-one ratio; balance among food choices, such as between leafy and pod vegetables, and between root vegetables and above-ground vegetables; and balance among and within your physical systems of circulation, assimilation, and elimination.

Many of the suggestions in the readings about managing your attitudes and emotions can be encapsulated as a series of parallel principles of balance—to choose constructive over nonconstructive thoughts, positivism over negativism, acceptance over judgmentalism, love over fear, and so on.

The advantage you have in achieving balance in your elder years is that you have had a range of experiences from which you can choose your options. One older woman I talked with put it this way:

These years are the fullest years for me. I may just be coming into the part of me that is really productive. In the years up to this, I've been getting all this experience, discovering what it's really all about, with all the satisfying in-the-marketplace sort of work that I've done—the physical work and even the mental work—so the spiritual side is just getting ready to have its day.

Because balance is a central theme of the Cayce philosophy and of achieving wisdom, you can use balance as a quick check on your progress as you apply the concepts and principles: How am I doing in keeping the physical, mental, and spiritual aspects in balance? Are work and relaxation balanced? How balanced are my thoughts about myself, about others, about the world around me? How balanced is my contribution to my health through diet? You may not be totally objective in answering such questions, but your willingness to look at your progress can be helpful in steering you away from extremes and back toward moderation and balance. The more often you check yourself with such questions, the more sensitive you become to what you are doing—and perhaps not doing.

The idea that the later years provide a prime time for achieving balances you have previously missed is supported by several of the writers and researchers referred to throughout this book. They also reinforce the concepts of realizing your wisdom and discovering the meaning of your life in your later years. Most notably, in *Vital Involvement in Old Age* Erik Erikson and his colleagues say that "the elder seeks to consolidate a sense of lifelong wisdom and perspective" trying to achieve a balance that tips in favor of integrity, rather than giving in to the opposing pull of despair. In his terms, integrity appears to be the satisfactory integration of all life experiences and understandings toward a realization and acceptance of the value and meaning of your life. Erikson declares that the strength of the elder is wisdom, following the succession of strengths in each of the preceding seven stages of life: hope, will, purpose, competence, fidelity, love, and care.

Your ability to maintain balance in your life is inherent in the will. That fact, coupled with the law that "the spirit is life, the mind is the builder, the physical is the result," can help you recognize that you are in control of your life, that you yourself determine your own circumstances. Such a realization places enormous responsibility on your shoulders; paradoxically, it is also a liberating concept and a potential source of tremendous satisfaction. Studies of the quality of life of older people suggest that those older than sixty who believe they control their lives have greater life satisfaction than those who believe their lives are controlled by luck, chance, fate, or other people. Control over your life contributes to successful aging.

What better time than now to understand your responsibility for your circumstances and to take initiative in controlling them? If you haven't directed your life to where you want it to go, if you haven't yet found meaning for your life, or if you're still looking for the wisdom of your years, it's not too late to find these elusive gifts. For they *are* gifts, waiting for you to recognize and accept them through your spiritual growth.

As a final inspiration to take up the charge, these truths paraphrased from the Cayce readings offer a prescription for a fulfilling life at any age:

Let the world be better for your having lived in it. Let those you meet day by day feel and know they are better for meeting and knowing and being with you. Keep loving if you would keep young. To be sure, there are various stages of unfoldment, of development, but use what you know to do and you will be given the next step. Those who seek to know themselves may find the way, and though the way be hard, those who find it become content, and find joy, peace, and happiness.

SELECTED
BIBLIOGRAPHY

American Association of Retired Persons. "How We Age." *AARP News Bulletin*, 28 (September 1987): 2.

Association for Research and Enlightenment. *A Search for God*. Vols. 1–3. Virginia Beach, Va.: A.R.E. Press, 1978 and 1982.

Berghorn, Forrest J., et al. *The Dynamics of Aging: Original Essays on the Processes and Experiences of Growing Old*. Boulder, Colo.: Westview Press, 1981.

Boyle, Sarah-Patton. *The Desert Blooms: A Personal Adventure in Growing Old Creatively*. Nashville: Abingdon Press, 1983.

Bro, Harmon H. *Dreams in the Life of Prayer & Meditation*. Virginia Beach, Va.: InnerVision Publishing Co., 1985.

Bro, Harmon H. "Toward a New World." *Venture Inward* 2 (July/August 1986): 44–45.

Christensen, Alice, and David Rankin. *Easy Does It Yoga for Older People*. San Francisco: Harper & Row, 1979.

Cousins, Norman. *Anatomy of an Illness as Perceived by the Patient: Reflections on Healing and Regeneration*. New York: W. W. Norton, 1979.

Cowley, Malcolm. *The View from Eighty*. New York: Viking Press, 1980.

Denton, Laurie. "Memory Subsystems in Precarious Balance." *APA Monitor* 23 (August 1987): 26.

Erikson, Erik H., Joan M. Erikson, and Helen Q. Kivnick. *Vital Involvement in Old Age*. New York: W. W. Norton, 1986.

Foundation for Inner Peace. *A Course in Miracles*. Vols. 1–3. Tiburon, Calif.: Foundation for Inner Peace, 1975.

Hallowell, Christopher. *Growing Old, Staying Young*. New York: William Morrow, 1985.

Hayes, Helen, with Marion Glasserow Gladney. *Our Best Years*. Garden City, N.Y.: Doubleday & Co., 1984.

Head, Joseph, and S. L. Cranston. *Reincarnation: The Phoenix Fire Mystery*. New York: Crown Publishers, Julian Press, 1977.

Hessel, Dieter. *Maggie Kuhn on Aging: A Dialogue*. Edited by Dieter Hessel. Philadelphia: Westminster Press, 1977.

Hoffer, William. "Aging: Destroying the Myths." *The Retired Officer* 43 (December 1987): 46–49.

Horn, Jack C., and Jeff Meer. "The Vintage Years." *Psychology Today* 21 (May 1987): 76–90.

Jung, C. G. *Memories, Dreams, Reflections*. New York: Vintage Books, 1965.

Justice, Blair. *Who Gets Sick*. Los Angeles: Jeremy P. Tarcher, 1988.

Kra, Siegfried. *Aging Myths: Reversible Causes of Mind and Memory Loss*. New York: McGraw-Hill, 1986.

LeShan, Eda. *Oh, to Be Fifty Again! On Being Too Old for a Mid-Life Crisis*. New York: Random House, Times Books, 1986.

Levinson, Daniel J., et al. *The Seasons of a Man's Life*. New York: Alfred A. Knopf, 1978.

Meer, Jeff. "The Reason of Age." *Psychology Today* 20 (June 1986): 60–64.

O'Regan, Brendan. "Spontaneous Remission: Studies of Self-Healing." *Noetic Sciences Review* (Spring 1988): 7–9.

Patent, Arnold. *You Can Have It All: The Art of Winning the Money Game and Living a Life of Joy*. Piermont, N.Y.: Celebration Publishing, 1984.

Peterson, Dick. "Eldercare: A Challenge in Service." *Venture Inward* 3 (September/October 1987): 34–37, 52.

Progoff, Ira. *At a Journal Workshop*. New York: Dialogue House Library, 1975.

Puryear, Meredith Ann. *Healing Through Meditation and Prayer*. Virginia Beach, Va.: A.R.E. Press, 1978.

Sheehy, Gail. *Passages: Predictable Crises of Adult Life*. New York: E. P. Dutton, 1976.

Simonton, O. Carl, Stephanie Matthews-Simonton, and James Creighton. *Getting Well Again*. Los Angeles: Jeremy P. Tarcher, 1978.

Solberg, Carl. *Hubert Humphrey: A Biography*. New York: W. W. Norton, 1984.

Thurston, Mark. *Discovering Your Soul's Purpose*. Virginia Beach, Va.: A.R.E. Press, 1984.

Thurston, Mark. *Dreams: Tonight's Answers for Tomorrow's Questions*. San Francisco: Harper & Row, 1988.

Thurston, Mark. *The Inner Power of Silence: A Universal Way of Meditation*. Virginia Beach, Va.: InnerVision Publishing, 1986.

Unity. *Foundations of Unity*, series 1 and 2. Unity Village, Mo.: Unity School of Christianity, 1973 and 1974.

INDEX

ABOUT THE
AUTHOR

In 1983 Dr. Richard Peterson began managing conferences and personnel for the Association for Research and Enlightenment (A.R.E.), the organization founded by Edgar Cayce. He left employment at the A.R.E. in 1988, in order to spend more time fulfilling home responsibilities and writing about the information in the Cayce readings.

He has a Ph.D. degree in organizational psychology. For more than twenty years he worked as a division manager for AT&T in New York and New Jersey, and most of his previous writing has appeared in business and professional publications. Dr. Peterson currently lives in Virginia Beach, Virginia.

EDGAR CAYCE'S
WISDOM FOR THE NEW AGE

More information from the Edgar Cayce readings is available to you on hundreds of topics, from astrology and arthritis to universal laws and world affairs, because Cayce established an organization, the Association for Research and Enlightenment (A.R.E.), to preserve his readings and make the information available to everyone.

Today over seventy-five thousand members of the A.R.E. receive a bimonthly magazine, *Venture Inward*, containing articles on dream interpretation, past lives, health and diet, psychic archaeology, and psi research, book reviews, and interviews with leaders in the metaphysical field. Members also receive extracts of medical and nonmedical readings and may do their own research in all of the over fourteen thousand readings that Edgar Cayce gave during his lifetime.

To receive more information about the association, which continues to research as well as make available information on subjects in the Edgar Cayce readings, please write A.R.E., Dept. M13, P.O. Box 595, Virginia Beach, VA 23451, or call (804) 428-3588. The A.R.E. will be happy to send you a packet of materials describing its current activities.